JB JOSSEY-BASS™
A Wiley Brand

T0314144

109 Ways to Retain Volunteers and Members

Scott C. Stevenson, Editor

WILEY

109 Ways to
Retain Volunteers & Members

Published by

Stevenson, Inc.

P.O. Box 4528 • Sioux City, Iowa • 51104
Phone 712.239.3010 • Fax 712.239.2166
www.stevensoninc.com

TABLE OF CONTENTS

TABLE OF CONTENTS

109 Ways to Retain Volunteers & Members.
Edited by Scott C. Stevenson.
© 2008 Stevenson, Inc. Published 2008 by Stevenson, Inc.

1 Invite Members To Beat the Dues Hike

Give your members the chance to "beat the dues hike." Set increases for membership dues several years in advance to encourage early renewals before the price hike.

Michael Sheward, president, Management Communications Strategies (Fairfax, VA), says nonprofit organizations should give their members at least two years notice when raising membership dues. Offer special deals for those who renew before the dues increase.

"To prepare current members for the dues hike, offer a two-year or multi-year renewal membership at current rates," says Sheward. Ensure that the multi-year offer overlaps or coincides with the first year of your new rates, so members can 'beat the dues hike,'" he says.

Member organization can benefit from planning in other ways. "When dues are paid forward in this fashion, those funds should be placed in a special, interest-bearing escrow account or CD, to be accessed only when the appropriate new dues year begins," Sheward says.

Source: Michael Sheward, President, Management Communications Strategies, Fairfax, VA. Phone (703) 218-2802. E-mail: shewardmcs@aol.com

2 Offer Volunteers A Relaxing Retreat

Do you find your volunteers suffering from burn out? To reenergize your volunteers, involve them in a volunteer retreat.

The Girl Scouts Council of Santa Clara County (San Jose, CA) offers their adult volunteers an annual three-day retreat. During the spring, any registered volunteer can attend Operation Relaxation.

Jacquie Peterson, committee chair, says volunteers travel to a nearby camp-like setting in the Santa Cruz Mountains where they relax while meeting old and new friends, receive great food, program activities and learning experiences to bring back to their troops. Volunteers can choose from an array of activities: yoga, massages, scrapbooking, enjoying the serenity of nature and more.

"Volunteers need to take care of themselves so they may continue to take care of others," says Peterson. "I have been an active volunteer in this council since 1964. If it weren't for Operation Relaxation, I would have burned out long ago."

Source: Jacquie Peterson, Operation Relaxation Committee Chair, Girl Scouts Council of Santa Clara County, San Jose, CA. Phone (650) 968-7211. E-mail: jacquie676@comcast.net

3 Connect Your CEO With Members

Creative communication may be key to increasing your executive director's visibility in the eyes of members.

"Every organization needs that representative figure who can provide a sense of confidence and trust, and share their vision for the institution," says Mary Jo Murphy, director of development, Berkshire Museum (Pittsfield, MA). "The more your members know him/her and hear from them in communications, the more these areas are made stronger, which results in more participation, financial support and increased retention."

Murphy says because of the museum's emphasis on member communications, they see an annual retention rate of 85 percent, and a 90 to 95 percent retention rate of their Crane Society (members contributing more than $1,000 annually).

To make himself more visible in members' eyes, the Berkshire's executive director:

1. **Writes personal notes.** The executive director reaches out to the museum's 2,700 household members by writing a letter in the organization's bi-monthly calendar and annual report. Once a year the director also sends a one-page informal letter to a group of 600 higher-level members to update them on current museum activities.

2. **Greets guests.** Prior to a new exhibit opening, the museum hosts a small gala where members get the chance to preview a new exhibit. The executive director stands in the lobby where he greets guests as they arrive, giving the director and guests a chance to meet and put faces with names.

3. **Hosts behind-the-scenes tours.** The development department creates small events where potential members and Crane Society members meet the executive director. The director leads the group of 12 to 20 individuals in a nearly two-hour, behind-the-scenes tour of the permanent collection storage areas.

Source: Mary Jo Murphy, Director of Development, Berkshire Museum, Pittsfield, MA. Phone (413) 443-7171. E-mail: mjmurphy@berkshiremuseum.org

4   Streamline the Renewal Process for Seasoned Members

Taking steps to make the renewal process less complicated for your members will be mutually beneficial. What's more, your members will value your efforts to make the process easier for them.

Darryl Walter, marketing manager, office of publishing and member services, American Association for the Advancement of Science (Washington, DC), says, "In the past we would send a renewal notice and ask members to fill out the member profile information. We now provide our members with the member profile data we have on file. We personalize it by lasering the variable date on the front of the renewal form. We ask members to update the data or fill in any missing data. We print the member profile data on the back of the form as a guide for members."

By updating the renewal process, you are taking the burden off your members and allowing them to renew their membership easily. This also enhances the membership experience and promotes members to renew year after year. Walter says, "By using variable data, we made the renewal process much easier for our members. They no longer have to fill in the demographic information every year. We also placed the privacy options on the front of the form to make it easier for members to update."

Source: Darryl Walter, Marketing Manager, Office of Publishing and Member Services, American Association for the Advancement of Science, Washington, DC. Phone (202) 326-6776. E-mail: dwalter@aaas.org

5   10 Ways to Show You Care

1. Write a thank-you note to a volunteer's spouse and/or children saying how much you appreciate the time their loved one has given you.

2. Invite volunteers of all ages to your recognition event and hold it when (nearly) everyone can come.

3. Put together a DVD of staff and clients saying "thanks" to volunteers. Premiere it at your recognition event and play it in your volunteer break room.

4. Track the dollar value of your volunteers' service and present them with a "mock" check at your annual recognition event.

5. As much as your schedule allows, check in on them as they are volunteering to offer words of thanks, a fresh cup of coffee or other type of "pat on the back."

6. Have volunteers invite a friend to the annual recognition event (this is also a recruiting tool as guests see how great your program is).

7. Recognize off-hour volunteers (persons who fill in evenings and weekends) with unexpected perks such as treats in the break room or a visit and hand shake from your CEO.

8. Thank your computer-savvy volunteers with a quick e-mail.

9. Every time one of your volunteers makes your organization's internal newsletter, print a copy of the article for your volunteer.

10. If appropriate for your organization, say thanks in a silly way! Ideas:

- Slap smiley-face stickers on volunteers' lapels or grab a colorful bouquet of flowers at the supermarket to add boutonnieres to volunteer uniforms to brighten everyone's day.

- Fill a cooler with ice cream bars and deliver to on-duty volunteers (be sure to include sugar- and fat-free choices).

- Hand out helium balloons with a handwritten note of thanks and a small bag of candy attached.

6   Spread Kindness With 'Secret Pals'

Want to spread a little kindness and cheer among volunteers? Why not create "secret pals?"

Whoever wants to participate fills out a form with general information about themselves (hobbies, interests, favorite candy or colors, etc.). One person collects the forms, then gives each form to a different person. Everyone then has a secret pal they do things for (e.g., give gifts, leave notes or just about any kind gesture you can think of). You know who you're doing nice things for, but they don't know who is doing it for them.

At the end of the year, have a little party. Reveal who everyone's secret pal is, and then start all over again.

Use this as team-building exercise and include paid staff, too.

7 Annual Feedback Form Results in More Service Hours

An annual feedback evaluation form for Pikes Peak Hospice & Palliative Care (Colorado Springs, CO) serves as an efficient tool to motivate and retain volunteers.

As a hospice standard of practice to evaluate volunteers annually, Pikes Peak Hospice staff developed the form to assess volunteer performance factors such as dependability, availability, judgment, attendance and following procedures.

The form, first sent to volunteers for self-evaluation, is based on a simple rating system of "S" for satisfactory performance or "O" for opportunities for improvement.

Once volunteers complete the self-evaluation, feedback is gathered from staff who work with the volunteers. Items such as volunteer achievements or requirements not fulfilled are also noted on the form.

Cathy Woods, director of volunteer services, then schedules a meeting with the volunteer at an off-site location, such as a coffee house, to discuss what was written by the volunteer and staff, plus additional thoughts from the volunteer services office.

For areas where there is room for improvement, Woods and the volunteer discuss a plan of action. She says the meetings are also a chance for volunteers to voice concerns and discuss if they should continue in their present assignment.

The feedback method helps volunteers, Woods says. Following a feedback session, she notes, they experience a 10 percent average increase in volunteer hours.

"Our retention rate for volunteers has also risen from an average of 1.8 years of service in 2003 to 3.6 years of service in 2007," she says. She attributes the increase to the feedback as well as having additional coordinators working with volunteers, more emphasis on interviewing and orientation, and improved continuing education classes.

Source: Cathy Woods, Director of Volunteer Services, Pikes Peak Hospice & Palliative Care, Colorado Springs, CO.
Phone (719) 633-3400, ext. 603.
E-mail: cwoods@pikespeakhospice.org

"Content not available in this edition"

8 Ask Paid Staff to Offer Encouraging Words

Involving staff is one surefire way to motivate your volunteers.

Mary Forti, volunteer coordinator, Women's Resource Center (Radford, VA), involved staff in the motivation of their volunteers at a staff in-service. At the monthly meeting, staff listened to a volunteer services PowerPoint presentation and then were given thank-you cards and asked to write a note of praise/thanks to one specific volunteer and deliver it within the next week.

"This was an excellent opportunity for paid staff to focus on the good things volunteers do for our organization," says Forti. "The personalized note gave each volunteer tangible proof of his/her importance."

Forti says in a 45-minute period, the organization sent a clear, consistent message: Volunteers are valuable, volunteers are a force for good and volunteers deserve respect.

> *"Volunteers are valuable, volunteers are a force for good and volunteers deserve respect."*

Source: Mary Forti, Volunteer Coordinator, Women's Resource Center, Radford, VA. Phone (540) 639-1123.
E-mail: volunteers@wrcnrv.org

9 How to Offer Discounts for Multi-year Renewals

Not sure whether to offer discounts to attract and retain members? Michael Soon Lee, president, EthnoConnect (Dublin, CA), says many factors should be taken into consideration before proceeding.

"Studies show the biggest membership loss to non-profits is at renewal time, because the notice is a reminder to question the value of the organization," says Lee. "To increase retention, consider offering a discount for multiple year renewals."

Lee addresses offering discounts to attract and retain members:

How should an organization determine the right discount?

"Many groups offer a 10 percent total discount for a two-year renewal, and a 15 percent total discount for a three-year renewal. However, you must compute the increase in retention rate, plus the decrease in billing costs to determine the break-even point. Obviously, you do not want to lose money by multi-year discounting."

Should membership discounts be offered to attract new members?

"These discounts lower the value of the organization and the value of the other members who paid full price. New member discounts insult those who have been loyal to the organization for a long time.

"Instead, offer new members a 'Special Report' that is appropriate to the group's purpose. For instance, a medical-related organization could offer tips on nutrition or resources in a special section of their website."

How should organizations handle pricing lifetime memberships?

"Compute the average length of membership, double it and multiply this figure by your current annual dues. This should

more than cover the cost of services provided." Lee says an effective retention strategy is to offer a lifetime membership for 10 to 20 times the annual fee."

Is there a way organizations can determine if their membership prices are too high?

Remember, you want to always have a solid return on your members' money, if you want to continue to do good work in the world. Nonprofits should examine similar organizations and find out their membership dues and benefits. Analyze whether your organization is competitive enough, he says. "This does not mean you must be cheaper than the other organizations. But if your dues are substantially higher, you must offer greater value and let your members know what that is."

Should organizations reduce membership prices?

"It's more effective to hold the price, until the market catches up to it. However, do try to increase the value of your memberships."

Source: Michael Soon Lee, President, EthnoConnect, Dublin, CA. Phone (800) 417-7325. E-mail: info@ethnoconnect.com

10 Sell Your Board On Volunteers' Importance

- Help your board understand the important role that volunteers play in your organization's work by having a volunteer make a brief presentation at each regularly scheduled board meeting. This also serves as a great way to recognize key volunteers' accomplishments.

11 Influence Member Renewals

People consider whether to renew memberships year-round, not just when the invoice comes, so be sure each experience they have with your organization is a positive one, says Rhoda Weiss, chair and CEO, Public Relations Society of America (PRSA) of New York, NY.

Weiss recommends:

- **Creating a "best practices" library.** If your association has many chapters, districts, regions and/or special interest sections, share stories online of successful member recruitment or communications programs. Read about what worked and didn't. Share your stories, too.

- **Involving members in recruitment.** In PRSA, local chapters search the media for names of new PR professionals. Invite these newcomers to your organization and ask them for names of co-workers who may be interested in joining your organization. Offer rewards for bringing in the most new members.

- **Giving discounts.** Offer coupons for prospects to attend events at low or no cost, and a lower dues structure initially for new professionals and recent college graduates.

- **Celebrating senior members.** "Tap into their wisdom by asking them to serve in a mentorship group, speak on panels of experienced professionals at a program, facilitate a workshop, judge awards competitions or scholarships and more," Weiss says. "Match their passion to the particular project." And remember that recognition goes a long way.

- **Creating a sense of community** with in-person groups, e-groups, casual gatherings, etc. "No matter the association, members rate networking as one of the most important benefits of organizational meetings," Weiss says.

- **Surfing the Internet** to learn about other organizations' recruitment, retention and promotional activities.

Source: Rhoda Weiss, Chair & CEO, Public Relations Society of America, New York, NY; and President, Rhoda Weiss & Associates, Santa Monica, CA. Phone (310) 393-5183. E-mail: Rhoda.weiss@prsa.org

12 Parking Decals Serve as Membership Badge of Honor

Providing members with parking decals not only makes identifying members easier, but it also can serve as a marketing tool and renewal reminder for members.

"Content not available in this edition"

"Since we are a land trust organization, the parking decals indicate to us and others using our preserves if someone is a member," says Holly Meeks, membership and special events, Lake Forest Open Lands Association (Lake Forest, IL). "Most importantly, no one is allowed to walk dogs in our preserves unless they're a member, which would only be indicated in the parking area with cars displaying a Lake Forest Open Lands decal."

Providing decals of this kind enables your members to be identified easily by your organization and community members. It's also a great way for members to show their commitment to your organization. "I think people almost view the decal as a 'badge of honor' for their involvement with an environmental organization on a local level. In addition, when non-members see the number of cars with decals parked at the entrance of a preserve, it gets them thinking about the importance of the land, the happiness it brings and the importance of conservation for future generations and hopefully encourages them to support the organization by joining," Meeks says.

Decals can be used for various reasons and convey different messages depending on your organization's growth. "Our logo has become very recognizable through the decals. It also has allowed us to project a special message such as this year's 40th anniversary message. On a more pragmatic note, it reminds members when their membership expires and to expect renewal invoices."

Source: Holly Meeks, Membership and Special Events, Lake Forest Open Lands Association, Lake Forest, IL. Phone (847) 234-3880, ext. 10. E-mail: hmeeks@lfola.org

13 Ask Volunteers How They Want to Be Recognized

Put out a suggestion box for recognition ideas. Ask volunteers to submit and sign ideas on how they personally would like to be recognized. You many not be able to fulfill everyone's wish, but will surely get an idea of what appeals to them.

14 Restructured Training Improves Volunteer Retention

Volunteers are introduced to numerous facets of your program through the training process. Danilo Minnick, director of volunteer services and student recruitment, Literacy Partners (New York, NY), notes that a restructured training program can help improve volunteer retention.

In 2002, only 19 percent of his volunteer tutor trainees met the required one-year commitment. Once the Literacy Partners application process was streamlined and the training process improved, 40 percent remained active for one to two years and 13 percent volunteered two or more years.

The number of volunteer "red flags" has also decreased, retention of trainees is between 90 and 95 percent, tutored students demonstrate greater educational gains, and the training program received national accreditation by ProLiteracy America (making it the only adult literacy program in New York City to receive this distinction).

Training sessions were previously held on an unscheduled basis, which made it more difficult to fill the meetings with qualified volunteers; a poorly written training manual didn't prepare volunteers for the tasks at hand. The schedule, resources and training structure have been changed. Four-week quarterly sessions were established. The committee also revised and divided the training manual into sections: teaching strategies, reading, writing, math and resources. New teaching practices give trainees more hands-on experience, including working in groups, on-site observations and making a presentation at the end of the training session. Volunteers provided immediate positive feedback once these changes were in place.

Volunteers also offer suggestions for further improvements in the training process. Their suggestions, which help keep the training relevant and timely, are also a catalyst for change.

Sources: Danilo Minnick, Director of Volunteer Services & Student Recruitment, Alexa Titus, Director of Education, Literacy Partners, New York, NY. Phone (212) 715-9200.
E-mail: danilom@literacypartners.org

15 What Does It Take to Get an E-zine Up and Running?

Looking for more cost-effective ways to communicate with members? Consider an *e-zine* — a periodic publication that you e-mail or post online.

Staff with the San Diego Regional Chamber of Commerce (San Diego, CA) established a monthly e-zine, *Business Online*, three years ago, says Scott Alevy, vice president of public policy and communications. "We needed to be able to communicate with our membership at a lower cost and in a way where they would be able to receive something at their desk."

Alevy outlines the steps involved:

1. **Inform your members.** Let members know you will be doing an online newsletter and give them the opportunity to opt out if they wish.

2. **Investigate which software is compatible with your system.** The chamber uses Contribute software ($300) to develop the e-zine.

3. **Select a mass e-mailing system.** The chamber uses the Cooler software to compose e-mails that send the e-zines to its constituents.

4. **Establish a story basis.** Decide which direction you want your e-zine to go and select stories that achieve that direction.

5. **Divide e-zine into categories.** Simplify the e-zine by segmenting it by topic (e.g., upcoming events, feature story, updates from various chamber offices, member spotlights, sponsorship links, benefits, etc.).

6. **Send out the publication.** Alevy says the chamber distributes the monthly e-zine to 5,500 subscribers. As part of the e-zine, the chamber allows recipients to forward the publication by e-mail. "There's really no telling how many thousands of people beyond our constituents view the e-zine," he says. "At a minimum I would say it gets in front of twice as many people as we send it to."

Source: Scott Alevy, Vice President of Public Policy and Communications, San Diego Regional Chamber of Commerce, San Diego, CA. Phone (619) 544-1360.
E-mail: salevy@sdchamber.org

16 Promptly Acknowledge New Members

Don't allow too much time to pass before officially acknowledging and welcoming new members to your ranks. Make a point to get a personal letter out to any new member within 48 hours of receipt of membership. This demonstrates your professionalism and underscores the value of the person's membership.

Additionally, list all new members in your official newsletter or magazine.

17 Report Helps Monitor, Evaluate Volunteer Commitment

Whether you track individual volunteer involvement through a particular software program, manually, or both, it's helpful to monitor and review individual volunteers' activities with your organization. Knowing what a volunteer has been doing during the past month (or quarter), how much time he/she has put into serving your cause and when, can provide you with useful clues and information including but not limited to these points:

1. If a volunteer's average monthly or quarterly hours are diminishing over time, his/her interest may be waning, and you can take steps to get at the root of the problem.

2. If a volunteer's time is distributed among a number of different activities, that may be an indication that he/she is trained in a number of areas and capable of taking on higher-level responsibilities.

3. Recognizing that a volunteer consistently volunteers at the same time on a daily, weekly or monthly basis alerts you to his/her preference regarding when and for how long he/she prefers to help your organization. Knowing that allows you to save certain tasks for those time slots.

4. In addition to making judgments about individual volunteers, you can also look for group statistics from which you may draw certain conclusions — if, for instance, a high number of volunteers is showing up on a particular day consistently or if a certain project attracts a larger than usual number of volunteers.

It's not enough to simply monitor volunteer activities and level of involvement. To make that tracking worthwhile, you need to be able to evaluate the data and draw worthwhile conclusions that impact your future management decisions.

MONTHLY VOLUNTEER ACTIVITY/ INVOLVEMENT REPORT

For the month of _____

Completed by _____

Volunteer	Date	Duration	Activity	Comments

18 Some Rewards Should Include Volunteer's Spouse, Family

As you consider rewards for a volunteer who has put in many hours for a special project, be mindful of the person's spouse and family as well. After all, the volunteer's absence from home may have involved sacrifice on the part of other family members.

Some ideas that reward the spouse/family include:

- A weekend getaway with paid hotel and tickets to the zoo or a performance.

- A visit by a professional house cleaning or carpet cleaning service to give a well-deserved break from cleaning.

Many of these rewards or incentives could be secured through donations.

19 Use Name Tags at Meetings

If you have a group of volunteers who may not know one another who meet from time to time, make up name tags they can wear at each meeting. Have them available at a table as they enter the meeting and ask that they return their badges at the conclusion of the meeting so they are available next time.

Here's another idea: Add a star or some other symbol to members' badges for recognition of some accomplishment — perfect attendance, great idea of the month, contributed hours or years of service. The various symbols on individuals' badges will add meaning to them and point out accomplishments.

20 Express Appreciation With a Letter to the Editor

Marc Jordan, president and CEO, United Way of Central Virginia (Lynchburg, VA), expressed appreciation to more than 1,700 volunteers for their contribution to the annual "Day of Caring" by sending a letter to the editor. A letter to the editor is a simple way to publicly thank volunteers, while describing your mission and acknowledging sponsors.

Jordan's letter to the *Lynchburg News and Advance* focused on the community impact of the Day of Caring event.

He also acknowledged major sponsors by name and asked readers to visit their facilities. Copies were sent to each sponsor, while volunteers could share their success with family and friends.

Source: R. Marc Jordan, President & CEO, United Way of Central Virginia, Lynchburg, VA. Phone (434) 455-6901. E-mail: marc.Jordan@unitedwaycv.org

21 Match Skills, Strengths to the Right Position

Gathering as much information as possible about your volunteers' interests can make matching your volunteers to the right positions much easier. Your volunteers will also be happier knowing their skills are being put to good use.

Y. Franklin Ishida, director for leadership development and mission personnel recruitment, Evangelical Lutheran Church in America (ELCA) in Chicago, IL, says the ELCA places volunteers based on a set of specific needs requested by churches and institutions in other parts of the world, so it's imperative to match a volunteer's skills with the position that needs to be filled.

The organization uses a volunteer request form to decipher what volunteer skills the hosting church body will need. The form not only includes the skills/qualities needed, but also a position description, benefits and length of service. Once a position is requested, the organization uses detailed volunteer applications to find a possible match.

Like most application forms, the ELCA's form asks questions about skills, interests and the desired area of service. But, to get more information about those skills, many questions are left in an open-ended, essay format and are separated by occupation, job-related skills, other skills or abilities and any professional licenses or certificates.

Once the ELCA has the information, a follow-up phone conversation elicits more information about what the volunteer can do and what the volunteer wants to do. "We usually seek a phone conversation, not as an interview, but as a way of talking directly and getting a better sense."

If the volunteer position will be long term, the volunteer is brought in for a daylong interview process. "It involves not just an interview with a three-person team (which includes the program director for the country/region of service), but also conversations with other staff in regards to missionary support and global mission education. We see the process to be one of 'discernment' rather than like a 'job interview.'"

The application also asks for references, which are used as another check into the volunteer's skills. Ishida says once they have all the information they need, they place the volunteer.

Source: Y. Franklin Ishida, Director for Leadership Development and Mission Personnel Recruitment, Evangelical Lutheran Church in America, Global Mission, Chicago, IL. Phone (773) 380-2700. E-mail: franklin.ishida@elca.org

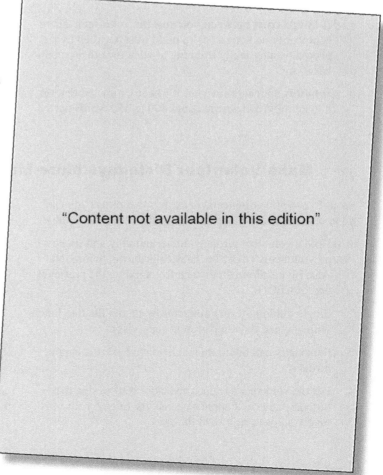

"Content not available in this edition"

22 Turn a General Meeting Into a Party

Usually meetings aren't the most exciting things for volunteers to attend, but that's not the case for Glencroft Retirement Community's (Glendale, AZ) general meeting/cow-themed party, "Holy Cow…we have the greatest volunteers!"

Every year Barb Lenards, director of community services, invites her 280 volunteers to attend the general meeting and volunteer board member election — usually about 80 attend.

So she decided to couple the meeting with a second volunteer appreciation event. "We started pushing the fun aspect of the meeting while saying 'by the way, we're going to elect officers,'" says Lenards.

The theme, which volunteers went nuts over and were talking about a week later, all started with cow-themed pins

Lenards found in Baudville catalogs and snowballed from there. Lenards found cow balloons, napkins and tablecloths. She contacted a local dairy and got cow baseball caps, mugs and pencils. She searched online and found cow suckers, slippers, towels and a cow-themed trivia game. Absolutely every decoration and recognition gift included the cow theme.

Lenards credits the theme for the higher attendance of 150. "I think the theme really did attract people. We felt it was important for the volunteers to come to the meetings so they can feel like they're part of something," she says.

Source: Barb Lenards, Director of Community Services, Glencroft Retirement Community, Glendale, AZ. Phone (623) 847-3004. E-mail: barb@glencroft.com

23 Listen to Your Volunteers

It's been said that we have two ears and one mouth and we should use them in that proportion. Three distinct benefits to listening to your volunteers:

1. **It builds trust between you and the volunteer.** There is probably no better way to build trust between two people than by really listening to what the other person has to say.

2. **It builds character in you.** It's been estimated that the human mind can absorb about 400 to 450 words per

minute. The average person speaks at about 100 to 150 words per minute. That means that the listener's mind has a lot of time to wander during the average conversation. Developing the skills necessary to really concentrate on what your volunteer is saying builds your own character.

3. **It builds self-esteem in the volunteer.** When you listen intently to what a volunteer has to say, it makes that person feel worthwhile, adding to his/her self-confidence.

24 Make Volunteer Birthdays More Memorable

From five to 500 volunteers, here are some things you can do to help make each individual birthday more memorable:

1. Hold a volunteer birthday dinner monthly and invite all volunteers whose birthday falls during that month. Also invite administrative staff, including the president and/or CEO.

2. Single out long-term volunteers by taking them to lunch with you and their department supervisors.

3. Personally call board members to wish them a happy birthday.

4. Get the volunteer's friends and close staff to sign the birthday card or, if applicable, ask the clients your volunteer helps to sign/send the card.

5. Post a blog on your website where friends, family and staff can post happy birthday messages to the volunteer.

6. Invite family members to come and celebrate the volunteer's birthday with you and your organization.

7. For monthly newsletters, print baby pictures of the volunteers' celebrating birthdays along with their names with a "Guess Who's Celebrating" caption.

Sources: Robin Popik, Volunteer Resources Supervisor, City of Plano, Plano, TX. Phone (972) 941-7114. E-mail: robinp@plano.gov
Judy Swinson, Director, Volunteer Services, St. Mary's Good Samaritan Inc., Mount Vernon, IL. Phone (618) 241-1031. E-mail: judy-swinson@ssmhc.com

25 Plan a Volunteer Retreat

Volunteer retreats are a great way to energize, motivate and recognize volunteers.

For 10 years Vicky Oboy, extension agent, Ohio State University Extension, Carroll County (Carrollton, OH), has been planning retreats for her 4-H volunteers. About 80 percent of her volunteers attend these retreats.

Each retreat, held at a conference center, includes: a theme; a fun opening session; an informative general session; two breakout sessions; lunch and the annual recognition event.

Breakout sessions have included topics for experienced volunteers, basics for new volunteers and specific help with finances, special projects and working with families. Every fall, Oboy sends a survey asking the volunteers what topics they want addressed. Once the topics are chosen, usually four, Oboy recruits extension professionals and 4-H volunteers from other states and counties to come and teach the sessions. Through registration materials, volunteers have the option to choose which breakout sessions would best help them.

Evaluations are given at the beginning of the retreat and are to be filled out during the day. The form asks what the volunteers thought about the sessions, theme, location, etc. Oboy says through this evaluation, they can determine what went well, what didn't and what changes need to be made for next year. To prove the retreat is effective, the form asks if the volunteers could use the information they learned. Recently 92 percent of volunteers said yes.

In fact, the success rates for the retreats have been so great that Oboy and staff decided to add the annual recognition ceremony to the agenda. "We used to do a banquet, but it started to lose attendance. Since we already had almost everyone at the retreat, we decided to incorporate it."

Source: Vicky Oboy, Extension Agent, The Ohio State University Extension, Carroll County, Carrollton, OH.
Phone (330) 627-4310. E-mail: oboy2@ag.osu.edu

Retreat Agenda

Vicky Oboy shares the agenda for her volunteer retreat:

9 a.m. — Opening session. Includes a fun icebreaker, skit or game to go along with the theme. Includes a general session, which explains what's happening with the county and 4-H.

10 a.m. — Breakout sessions. Two breakout sessions cover about four topics that address the needs of the volunteers. Volunteers pick which topics are relevant to them.

Noon — Luncheon. Volunteers listen to a speaker, usually an extension professional, who talks about something relevant to the entire group.

1 p.m. — Recognition ceremony. Awards are given for attendance and to outstanding volunteers.

26 Key Components for Position Descriptions

Some nonprofits make the mistake of classifying all volunteers under one job category and then varying their assignments and expectations. The result is volunteers not quite sure about what's expected of them.

Having a description for each volunteer position will eliminate that confusion. Be sure each description includes the following components:

Job Title — Avoid a general title such as *office volunteer.* Instead, come up with a specific and meaningful title, such as *newsletter production member.*

Date — The date the description was written or last updated to serve as a reminder to review the description occasionally and update it as needed.

Description Summary — A one- or two-sentence description that captures the essence of the position.

Qualifications — Be as specific as necessary, including *minimum* qualifications, not ideal ones.

Job Duties/Activities — This is a list of specific tasks to be performed, perhaps categorized under like headings.

Working Conditions — Indicate if the job involves hazardous conditions, outside or strenuous work, etc.

Conditions of Service — Is reliable transportation necessary? Does the organization reimburse transportation and parking costs? Is a uniform provided? Are meals provided? Are there any other benefits or considerations that a volunteer should know about?

Supervision — Volunteers need to know who their immediate supervisors are and where those persons fit within the organization. Problems can quickly arise if a volunteer doesn't know who to approach with questions or from whom he/she should take direction.

27 Pairing Up Volunteers Has Its Advantages

Ever consider pairing up volunteers? For officials with Make-A-Wish Foundation® of Metro New York (Lake Success, NY), the decision to match volunteers with one another came down to partnership, safety and flexibility.

"The whole concept behind the pairing of volunteers is *partnerships*," says Maria Casey, director, volunteer services. "When volunteers work together, they're learning from each other and have someone to bounce their ideas off. That in turn results in responsibility and accountability."

With the majority of the volunteer's work conducted in the field, Casey says it's best for the volunteers' safety to never be alone on an assignment. This pairing also allows for flexibility, which enables tasks to continue in case one volunteer is unable to attend an assignment.

The organization has paired volunteers in the areas of wish granting, public speaking and fundraising events through its mentor/trainee program for more than 15 years. Casey estimates one-third of the organization's 700 volunteers work in pairs.

Before pairing volunteers, Casey considers the mentor's:

- **Experience.** "We ask ourselves, 'Is the potential mentor experienced and would they be a great fit with the new recruits?'" Casey says to determine a great fit, the organization considers the volunteer's involvement in various projects. Casey says possessing a depth of knowledge about the organization is also required.

- **Communication.** Potential mentors' communications skills are evaluated to determine their capability in answering new recruit questions.

- **Availability.** The mentor's current workload is analyzed to see if they can take on a new volunteer.

Source: Maria Casey, Director, Volunteer Services, Make-A-Wish Foundation® of Metro New York, Lake Success, NY. Phone (516) 944-6212, ext. 105. E-mail: mcasey@metrony.wish.org

28 How to Praise A Volunteer

Giving praise to a volunteer may seem like a simple action, but there are some guidelines to follow when giving that praise to make it more meaningful:

1. **Be specific.** Praising a volunteer in general terms and every time he/she performs a simple task may seem insincere and trite. But praise that volunteer for a specific job and it will mean much more. Always praise specific actions you want to see repeated. For example: "You did a very thorough job answering your tour group's questions. Having such a knowledgeable volunteer as yourself on board is a great asset."

2. **Be intermittent.** Studies have shown praise means more when it's not expected. Give your praise intermittently and not on a continuous basis where it might grow tiresome to the volunteer receiving it.

3. **Be immediate.** The closer the praise is to the action being commended, the better the chances that action will be repeated.

29 Offer a Sabbatical To Deserving Volunteers

Colleges and universities, even some companies, have offered sabbaticals — an extended period of leave from one's customary work — to deserving faculty and employees for years. They're offered as a "rest" or an opportunity to acquire new skills.

Why not use the sabbatical concept for volunteers who have served your organization for a long period, as a way to give them a deserved break?

Here's one scenario of how a volunteer sabbatical might work.

1. To give your sabbatical the importance it deserves, limit them (e.g., one sabbatical per year or one sabbatical every six months).

2. Assign the selection of your sabbatical recipient to a committee who can review a list of deserving nominees.

3. Announce the sabbatical recipient(s) at your annual volunteer recognition event.

4. Get one or more businesses to sponsor your sabbatical program by underwriting any costs associated with it. Some of those costs might include:
   - A cash honorarium and/or gift for the sabbatical recipient.
   - The cost of the actual award to be given to the recipient.
   - The cost associated with some educational opportunity for the recipient.
   - Possible travel expenses.

30 Tip Sheet Helps With Recruitment and Retention

At training sessions for volunteers, Esther Cantu, director, Agency and Volunteer Programs for the Volunteer Center at United Way of San Antonio and Bexar County (San Antonio, TX), gives out tip sheets they can refer to for volunteer recruitment and retention.

Explaining the origin of the tip sheets, Cantu says, "I had to develop a presentation on recruiting volunteers and I used information that made sense to me and that I had come across in daily routine."

The tips tell how to engage, motivate and connect with volunteers based on the volunteer's motivation: power, affiliation or achievement.

Cantu explains that a *power-motivated volunteer* wants a position of power or leadership, such as a board or committee post. An *affiliation volunteer* likes to socialize while he/she volunteers, while an *achievement-motivated volunteer* is interested in awards and recognition.

She says she has also seen and heard about other volunteer coordinators putting these tips into action. "It's a good handout because it's effective and easy to use and refer to." she says.

Source: Esther Cantu, Director, Agency and Volunteer Programs, The Volunteer Center at United Way of San Antonio and Bexar County, San Antonio, TX. Phone (210) 352-7099. E-mail: ecantu@unitedwaysatx.org. Website: www.unitedwayatx.org

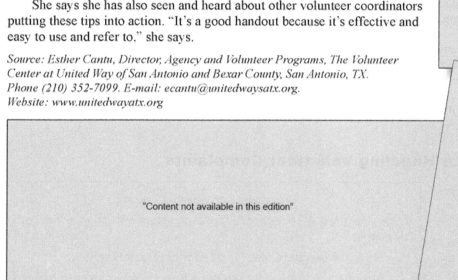

"Content not available in this edition"

"Content not available in this edition"

31 Frequency of Feedback Matters to Some Volunteers

We all need feedback in order to do our jobs effectively. What type of feedback and how often we need it vary from one individual to the next. Are you in tune with your volunteers' "feedback needs?"

If the No. 1 complaint about feedback is that managers give too little, the No. 2 complaint is that they give too much. Simply piling on more feedback isn't the answer. You need to tune in to the unique frequencies of each individual.

Be observant, listen and remain alert for opportunities to give volunteers feedback when they want and/or need it. Remember, one size doesn't fit all.

How frequently you give volunteers feedback should be based on:

- Their tasks and responsibilities
- The work they're producing
- The questions they ask
- The requests they make

The best managers look for the best feedback opportunities. You can't respond to everything, nor would you want to. So seize the feedback opportunities that work best for each person. And select the vehicle of communication that works best for each person, as well — e-mail, a face-to-face conversation, a memo or a telephone call.

32 Help 'Above & Beyond' Volunteers Get Noticed

Here's an idea to reward your volunteers for going above and beyond the call of duty while performing their jobs:

Make up simple forms with *Above and Beyond* at the top and a place to write a volunteer's name. Give them to staff members and when they see a volunteer doing something "above and beyond" the normal job requirements, have them fill out the form. Collect the forms and once a month choose one to receive a donated prize.

Innovation Industries, Inc., an Arkansas-based manu-facturer of elevator industry products, has a similar program called "Catch Me At My Best." Amber Dilday, administrative assistant there, says "We have forms to fill out on co-workers you 'catch' doing something that exceeds expectations. These are turned in monthly and the winner is given tickets for dinner for two and special parking for the month. At the end of the year we have the 'Best of Innovation' and all cards submitted throughout the year are entered into a drawing for a special prize."

33 Study Volunteers Who Stick With You

Do you *really* know why certain volunteers choose to remain active with your cause for a long period of time? By identifying a primary reason — your mission, the work environment, interaction with clients or other volunteers, etc. — you can use that knowledge in your marketing mix to attract new volunteers motivated by the same rationale.

To get an accurate reading on why volunteers have stayed with you, meet one-on-one with those who have been with you the longest. Ask them a series of questions that gets at the real reason for their long tenure with your agency. As you meet with each volunteer, see if a particular reason emerges as the most popular. If it does, you will have unlocked the secret to their long-term association with your cause. And once you know that, you can use that information to further retain volunteers and to attract new ones.

34 Have a Procedure for Handling Volunteer Complaints

Do you have a procedure for those instances in which a volunteer lodges a complaint? Having a written procedure:

1. Helps ensure that a volunteer's complaint will be heard and responded to by supervisors or others in authority.
2. Enables you to follow a consistent set of steps in an effort to remedy the perceived or real problem.
3. Helps to protect your organization in those instances in which the complaint could have far-reaching (even legal) ramifications.

Use this generic volunteer complaint template to develop your own.

Volunteer Complaint Procedures

Whenever a volunteer submits a formal complaint (in writing, in person or by phone):

1. Share the complaint with the director of volunteer services.
2. The director of volunteer services is responsible for meeting with the complainant to gather information.
3. After meeting with the complainant, the director of volunteer services shall put the complaint in writing and share it with appropriate staff.
4. The director of volunteer services will then investigate and, if possible, address the complaint.
5. The director of volunteer services will respond back to complainant (by writing, by phone or in person) within four weeks of receiving the complaint.
6. Having responded to the complainant, the director of volunteer services will produce a written summary of follow-up actions that took place following the complaint. Copies of the summary will be shared with the executive director, any staff involved with or affected by the complaint, placed in the complainant's file and placed in the Complaints file.

If the volunteer lodging the complaint is not satisfied with the actions taken, he/she may lodge the complaint with the executive director for further review and possible action.

---

35 Teen Incentive Program Increases Hours

Amy Krueger, junior volunteer assistant, St. Cloud Hospital (St. Cloud, MN), found a great incentive idea for her teen volunteers that she can do right in her hospital: She offers quarterly tours to junior volunteers who show up for 75 percent or more of the shifts they are required to have.

Since offering the tours, she's seen teens' volunteer hours increase by 14 percent.

That's because these aren't just any tours. No one else gets to see what these junior volunteers do, not visitors and not other volunteers, Krueger says.

"We really wanted it to just be their reward," says Krueger. Meaning while other tours may show the morgue, they don't get into the detail the incentive tours do, like visiting the lab too and examining body parts.

Teen tours have also included watching surgeries and visiting the helipad during a take-off or landing.

"We picked certain areas we knew would be interesting, things people normally don't get to see," she says.

The logistics were pretty easy to work out, she says. Since all hospital volunteers go through HIPAA patient confidentiality training and infection control education, it was really just about going to each department to work out the details. For instance, only six people are allowed on the helipad at a time. Since there are around 20 volunteers per tour, she split one group into three.

Krueger says she has a dedicated group of junior volunteers whose interests lie in the medical field and who always put in their hours (12 a month during the school year, 20 a month in the summer). But, she notes, a full 50 percent of her volunteers are new to the tour every quarter.

Source: Amy Krueger, Junior Volunteer Assistant, Director, Volunteer Services, St. Cloud Hospital, St. Cloud, MN.
Phone (320) 255-5638. E-mail: riedemanj@centracare.com

36 Displays That Recognize Volunteers' Contributions

Go beyond the traditional bulletin board with these ways to call attention to volunteers' contributions to your cause:

- **Public Video Presentation.** Create a permanent lobby display that can serve a variety of purposes to build your volunteer program. Use a DVD player to share a recording of volunteers at work, home and at volunteer duties.

- **Interactive Virtual Display.** Build a computer kiosk with a touch screen where visitors can select a topic and view a biographical sketch of volunteers, including facts and figures related to the impact they have on your organization. Provide a screen or post information of who to contact to become a volunteer.

- **Free Media.** Develop a partnership with local media outlets where you can submit a brief press release or public service announcement each month to announce a special volunteer. In return, recognize the media outlet as a sponsor of one of your community betterment projects.

- **Volunteer Scrapbook.** Even if your budget is small, you can create a scrapbook for every important volunteer you want to honor. Start one honoring another person each month, quarter or year, as budget and time allow (this would be an ideal project for a crafty volunteer). Ask friends and family for photos of milestones, including shots of the person volunteering. Use clippings, mementoes and certificates. Leave the book on display for visitors, staff and clients to enjoy before the honoree takes it home.

- **Multipurpose Display.** On a writing table or desk in your reception area, place a framed photo of a volunteer with the caption, "Why I Volunteer." Include personalized flyers in which the subject answers the question, along with information on where the person volunteers. Include a form to fill out to receive more information about volunteering, or have pens and a drop box so persons can complete the form on site. Change the display and story monthly.

37 Member Retention Tactics

To get current members to renew, be sure to include these three approaches in your arsenal of tactics:

1. **Offer "teasers" of what's to come.** As you approach the end of someone's membership, share a taste of what will be offered as new and exciting members-only benefits in the upcoming year.

2. **Make the renewing process simple as pie.** Take advantage of a mail-merge program that preprints membership forms to minimize what the member will need to complete.

3. **Don't give up on lapsed members.** Just because a renewal date has come and gone doesn't mean you should give up. Conduct a special phonathon effort to this group offering a "limited time" perk for renewing now.

38 Survey of Personal Interests Uncovers Special Opportunities

Are you aware of your volunteers' hobbies and special interests? How much do you know about those interests?

It's worth your time to learn more about each of your volunteers' special interests. Who knows when your awareness of a particular interest may be somehow used for volunteer purposes? Someone who collects butterflies, for instance, might be asked to give a presentation about the collection. Likewise, a volunteer who is into photography may be the perfect individual to take candid shots at an upcoming event. You never know where opportunities may arise to make use of volunteers' special interests.

To get more familiar with the hobbies and particular interests of your volunteers, invite them to complete a *personal interests survey* that you can keep on file. Depending on the number of volunteers with whom you work, you may even choose to create an index of interest categories that can be easily reviewed when a particular task calls for a particular set of interests.

Knowing your volunteers' special interests not only allows you to better match them with projects and tasks, but it has other benefits as well: Depending on their particular hobby, you can recognize individual volunteers on a weekly or monthly basis by displaying their collection for others to see. Those whose hobbies are showcased will be flattered and feel more appreciated than ever.

SPECIAL INTERESTS, HOBBIES INVENTORY

Name _____   Daytime Phone _____

Date Completed_____   E-mail _____

I would like to share with you my top special interests or hobbies. They include the following:

SPECIAL INTEREST/HOBBY NO. 1_____

Description of my interest/hobby _____

How long I have been doing it: _____

How I got started: _____

Why I enjoy it: _____

Any features about my hobby/interest/collection worth mentioning: _____

SPECIAL INTEREST/HOBBY NO. 2_____

Description of my interest/hobby _____

How long I have been doing it: _____

How I got started: _____

Why I enjoy it: _____

Any features about my hobby/interest/collection worth mentioning: _____

---

39 Launch a 'Member-of-the-Month' Program

Membership recognition can take on many forms. The Virginia Chamber of Commerce (Richmond, VA), for example, recognizes members through its member-of-the-month program.

"Our member-of-the-month program allows us to recognize and applaud members for their efforts as strong business leaders in Virginia," says Stephanie Pelletier, membership operations coordinator. "It also gives us the opportunity to showcase members, giving them visibility among other chamber members."

Vice President of Membership Sandy Harrell designed the member-of-the-month program more than 10 years ago. Currently honorees are chosen when the member company's name is selected from a drawing during regional events across the state throughout the year.

"The member-of-the-month program is another way to touch your members — giving them a chance to 'shine in the spotlight' for their dedication and commitment to your organization," says Pelletier.

Once chosen, the members are recognized with a small profile about their business on the chamber's website and in the chamber's e-newsletter, *Chamber Briefings*, which is viewed by more than 1,100 members.

For more information on Virginia Chamber of Commerce's member-of-the-month recognition, visit: www.vachamber.com.

Source: Stephanie Pelletier, Membership Operations Coordinator, Virginia Chamber of Commerce, Richmond, VA.
Phone (804) 237-1457. E-mail: s.pelletier@vachamber.com

40 Volunteer Committee Plans Training/Fulfillment Events

Staff at the Denver Museum of Nature and Science (Denver, CO), has put together a unique volunteer program to energize and motivate volunteers. It's called the Volunteer Enrichment Committee. The committee, made up of volunteers and three staff members, plans volunteer continuing education and fulfillment events from start to finish.

"Our volunteers are self-described 'lifelong learners,' so this program is tailored to them and produces results. Many of our volunteers spend years volunteering with us because of a myriad of learning opportunities available to them. The Volunteer Enrichment Committee is a big part of that volunteer longevity at DMNS," says Beth Kaspar, coordinator of volunteers for Prehistoric Journey and Hall of Life.

Here's how it works:

- 12 volunteers are handpicked for the committee.
- Volunteer committee members are required to: attend all meetings, serve at least three years and plan at least one event.
- Each August the committee outlines a yearlong calendar of events, plans at least 12 continuing education events and four enrichment events.
- Volunteers are notified about events through: the museum's computer check-in system, fliers, the volunteer newsletter, other specific newsletters and direct mail.
- Space limitations are set on an event-by-event basis.

Source: Beth Kaspar, Coordinator of Volunteers for Prehistoric Journey & Hall of Life, Denver Museum of Nature and Science, Denver, CO. Phone (303) 370-8344. E-mail: beth.kaspar@dmns.org

41 Thank Members With a Telephone Campaign

Host a thank-you campaign to directly tell your members you appreciate them.

Big Brothers Big Sisters of Greater Miami (Miami, FL) holds a telephone "Thank-You-Thon" twice a year, says Ryan Roth, development manager. Organizers hold the massive phone drive for one day at the end of the organization's fiscal year and again during the holiday season.

To prepare for the day-long outreach effort, staff first assemble a list of all the organization's donors. They divide the list equally — in groups of about 20 names — and distribute among match support staff to make personal phone calls. (Match staff members are involved in the success of the mentoring program. They're assigned to matches to help guide and plan activities for them.)

"This year (2007), we reached a record 2,000 matches,"

says Roth. "We used that as our 'good news' for calling to again reinforce how their dollars are helping us match more kids in the community and provide a mentor for them."

Callers are given sample scripts, which they then customize as they make calls to personally thank the donors for their support. They also receive a script designed to leave voice mail messages.

"The power of saying 'thank you' is forgotten a lot in our business," Roth says. "Most donors are very surprised to receive a call simply to say 'thanks.' Many of these calls have led to future donations and have really helped to keep our donors engaged in the program."

Source: Ryan Roth, Development Manager, Big Brothers Big Sisters of Greater Miami, Miami, FL. Phone (305) 644-0066.
E-mail: rroth@bbbsmiami.org

42 Find Everyday Ways to Salute Volunteer Achievements

Don't wait for an annual event to recognize your volunteers' achievements. Use record keeping, evaluations, trainings, recruitment and volunteer/employee relations to celebrate your volunteers all year long. For instance:

- **Take photos of your volunteers in action.** Post them online and on agency bulletin boards. Print them in newsletters. Show the many types of volunteers and the many activities they do to help your clients, visitors and staff.

- **Develop a "Volunteer Victory" alert form**, on paper or e-mail, and share successes as they happen. Include the names of paid support staff, too.

- **Submit reports that pass the "So-What?" test.** Make sure data is distributed to each department and to all volunteers themselves.

- **Keep a continuous testimonial and comment log.** Train yourself to listen to and log what people say about volunteers and their contributions.

- **Ask for special notes on excellent volunteer management** to be placed into employees' personnel records.

- **Initiate a "sudden praise squad"** — a team of people that descends with attention-getting fun upon a person who just achieved something. Leave a consistent reward behind like a special paperweight, framed medal, etc.

Source: Susan J. Ellis, President, Energize, Inc., Philadelphia, PA. Phone (215) 438-8342. E-mail: susan@energizeinc.com. Website: www.energizeinc.com

"Content not available in this edition"

A form like this can boost awareness of your volunteers. Post forms in a public area and share responses with volunteers and in your employee newsletter.

43 Ideas for Your Volunteer Recognition Event

Most volunteer-driven organizations hold a volunteer recognition event at least once each year. To make your event all that it can be:

- Incorporate a new theme into each year's event.

- Include number of years served on volunteers' name tags.

- Invite your board of directors to be present.

- Ask someone served by your agency to say a few words from the heart.

- Incorporate a higher level of recognition (e.g., lapel pin, special seating, etc.) for those who have served five years or more.

- Invite members of the audience to make individual toasts for special group or individual volunteer acts performed throughout the year.

- List all volunteers' names on the program in order of number of years served.

- Have your organization's CEO at the door or registration table, greeting volunteers as they arrive.

- Invite *emeritus* volunteers (those who have retired after years of service) to attend.

- Ask your employees to be present.

- Have those in attendance enter their names for a donated door prize to be given away.

- Incorporate lighthearted awards into your recognition (e.g., most times late for meetings, best excuse for showing up late for a volunteer duty).

- Get sponsors to underwrite the cost of a more upscale event.

- List the year's volunteer accomplishments in your program.

44 Five Ways to Support Committee Chairpersons

To be effective leaders, committee chairpersons need your full support. After all, these are the individuals who are assuming leadership for work that frees up your time. They are also the ones who set the example for other volunteers. Committee chairs need and deserve a level of attention that goes beyond that of grassroots volunteers.

To fully nurture your chairpersons:

1. **Provide them with special training.** Go over responsibilities in detail. Show them what has been done in the past. Share notes, minutes, budget details and other information so they are aware of what needs to happen. Give them a list of answers to "what-if" questions so they have some understanding of what to do or where to go when necessary.

2. **Treat them like paid staff.** Introduce them to other personnel and those you serve. Treat them with importance to help them recognize the importance of their positions.

3. **Help them realize the impact of their work.** Help them visualize how the successful completion of their work fits into the big picture. Know that their level of inspiration will motivate those who report to them or serve on their committees.

4. **Give them the perks they deserve.** If possible, provide office space or a location designated for higher-up volunteer managers. Periodically send brief notes of encouragement. Provide special attribution in recognizing their leadership in publications, during events, etc.

5. **Keep communication lines open.** Meet with committee chairpersons regularly to go over issues, plans and accomplishments to date. Encourage them to come to you with questions/concerns. Let them know how best to reach you (e.g., phone, e-mail or in person).

45 Recognition Program Celebrates 'Continuous' Membership

Send your members personal cards to mark special anniversaries — and to encourage their renewals.

The Association of Legal Administrators (ALA) of Lincolnshire, IL sends anniversary cards to members celebrating their first and fifth, as well as 10th, 15th 20th, 25th and 35th anniversaries.

"We recognize only continuous and uninterrupted membership, so this encourages members to be timely in renewing their memberships," says Debbie Curtis, director of membership.

A personal touch enhances the success of the recognition program. "The association president personally signs cards for all individuals with 25 or more years of continuous membership; this is approximately 200 cards," Curtis says. "The notes were of a personal nature and varied depending on whether the president knew the recipient."

They also used postage stamps for mailing the anniversary cards, rather than postage meters, to make them more personal. Approximately 2,500 cards were mailed in the project's first year.

Most members gave ALA positive feedback for their postcards. "Members really appreciated the recognition and the fact we took the time to acknowledge their achievement," Curtis says.

Negative feedback came from members who had a break in their service at some point. For example, ALA sent a five-year anniversary card to a member who had been with the organization off and on for 15 years. In those cases, the organization explained its "continuous and uninterrupted" requirement for anniversary recognition.

"The goodwill created far outweighed the limited negative feedback," Curtis says.

ALA hired a design company to create the cards and matching envelopes. Another company was hired to handle the printing and mailing. "The initial cost per card/envelope was $2 to $2.25, including postage," Curtis says. "This will be lower in future years, since the design costs (included in the card costs) are a one-time expense."

Source: Debbie Curtis, Director of Membership, The Association of Legal Administrators (ALA), Lincolnshire, IL. Phone (847) 267-1388. E-mail: dcurtis@alanet.org

46 Make Time For Creative Picnics

There's no time like summer to take a moment and tell your volunteers you care; and there's no better way to do so than with a picnic. To add some flare to your picnic, consider:

- Preparing a giveaway picnic basket for each attending volunteer that includes some surprises tailored to that individual.

- Asking community leaders (your mayor, others) to show up as a surprise and thank those present for their dedication.

- Arranging surprise entertainment — a musical ensemble, a storyteller or a woodcarver who can demonstrate his/her craft.

47 Get the Inside Scoop on Your Volunteer Program

Giving your volunteers formal assessment tools can help make improvements, detect volunteer burnout and provide positive reinforcement for staff.

Paula Pritchard, volunteer coordinator, Vision House (Renton, WA), recently added a *Volunteer Assessment of the Volunteer Program* Form.

"Our volunteer program is growing very quickly, and we needed a more formal way to stay on top of our volunteer's concerns, needs and suggestions," she says.

Forms are given to volunteers twice a year to help keep up with newcomers.

"I tell our volunteers that these forms are really helpful for us because as staff members, we have no way of knowing or understanding what it's really like to be a Vision House volunteer," says Pritchard.

By looking over the answers with the appropriate staff, she determines what changes need to be made and even whether to be on the lookout for burnout problems they've had in the past.

Plus, positive comments are a great morale booster, she adds: "I'll read them over sometimes if I'm feeling discouraged, or share them with appropriate staff members."

Pritchard gives a special form to new volunteers after their third volunteer experience to help identify and address any holes in orientation and training.

"Again, rather than assuming that they would come to me if there were any problems," the volunteer coordinator says, "I like to take a more proactive approach to making our volunteers' experience the best it can be."

Source: Paula Pritchard, Volunteer Coordinator, Vision House, Renton, WA. Phone (425) 228-6356. E-mail: paulap@vision-house.org

"Content not available in this edition"

48 Frequent 'Rituals' Help Formalize New Relationships

Any induction actions directed to an individual that he/she perceives as "official" tend to solidify that person's ties with the sponsoring organization. The actions may be in the form of a welcome letter or certificate of membership, the presentation of a lapel pin or a more formal ceremony of sorts.

To help strengthen new volunteers' ties to your cause, make use of "rites" or "rituals" they will find meaningful as they begin what will hopefully become lasting relationships with your organization. It may even be appropriate to carry out a series of such actions during the first weeks or months of their association with your agency.

Here are some examples of new member (or volunteer) induction measures:

- A letter of welcome from the executive director and/or board chairperson.

- Presentation of an official certificate of membership or association.

- An official induction ceremony with other members (or volunteers) present.

- An initiation or apprenticeship period.

- Presentation of some treasured memento — a lapel pin, a paperweight or book.

- Completing some act or ritual considered exclusive to official members or volunteers of the organization.

49 10 Ways to Under-promise and Over-deliver

You've heard it before: "Under-promise and over-deliver." It's a practice that makes a good deal of sense, but how often do you apply the rule in your daily work? Here are 10 ways that this principle works for volunteer managers:

1. Announce that a meeting will last no longer than 90 minutes and then finish it within an hour.

2. Overestimate the time it will take to get a community service project completed; then finish it in less time.

3. Suggest that a project will require more volunteers than is actually necessary.

4. Underestimate the net income that a new special event will generate, and then surprise your boss when it brings in far more than that amount.

5. Overestimate the costs associated with a new volunteer

project and then come in under budget.

6. Set a somewhat overly ambitious goal for a group of volunteers and then inform (and reward) them when they have achieved the actual goal you had in mind.

7. Promise a modest reward or incentive for any volunteer who meets your stated goal and then surprise that person with a bonus.

8. Explain to your new chairperson what will be required of him/her and then make the job easier than was originally explained.

9. Offer to lend a hand and then do more than expected.

10. Offer more praise, give more training and provide more support and recognition than a volunteer is accustomed to receiving.

50 Don't Lose Volunteers To High Gas Prices

Are you faced with the prospect of losing volunteers because of soaring gas prices? The following tactics can help reduce the squeeze on your volunteers' wallets:

- Ask local businesses to sponsor one or more volunteers by purchasing their gas for the next year with a gas card. You can also ask local gas stations to make a donation by providing gas credits to your volunteers.
- Reimburse volunteers for mileage or establish a monthly stipend.
- Post a carpooling sign-up sheet in your volunteer office, break room, etc.
- If appropriate, consider having the volunteer work from home (e.g., data entry, preparing mailings, etc.).

51 Be Wary of Too Much Volunteer Isolation

Be mindful of the degree to which volunteers work in isolated environments. Though some volunteers may be more introverted than others and prefer the solitude, it's important to:

- Keep tabs on their accomplishments.

- Let them know that someone is available to assist them if necessary.

- Be assured that their behavior is normal in spite of their comfort at working in isolated circumstances.

- Offer words of recognition and encouragement from time to time.

52 Incentive Program Motivates Volunteers

Officials with the Lee County Parks and Recreation (Ft. Myers, FL) have established a Volunteer Incentives program to help motivate their 1,100 volunteers.

Kathy Cahill, volunteer services coordinator, says in 2003 they implemented the incentives program to award members for their contributions to the county.

The program allows volunteers to accumulate their hours to "purchase" the item(s) of their choice from a four-page catalog. Items include: sports-pro binoculars with case (300 hours); no-spill travel mug (35 hours); AM/FM portable radio with earphones (45 hours); talking pedometer (200 hours); cooler/lunch bag (80 hours); golf shirt (200 hours); parking pass sticker (40 hours); and pool passes and classes (40 to 80 hours). Volunteers can also save their hours from year to year and/or combine their hours with fellow volunteers.

Cahill says the parking pass, which allows volunteers to park at all parks, boat ramps and beach access points free for one year, has become the most popular item. Because of its popularity, volunteers who have accumulated 40 hours can choose the parking pass and still keep their 40 hours to be used or saved to "purchase" another item.

"The volunteers absolutely love the program," says Cahill. "Not only can they receive items but they can also use it for Christmas shopping. Because every item has our name and logo on it, it has become a great way for us to get more publicity."

The items which are purchased at a minimal cost of cents on the dollar to $25 for a special order golf shirt are worth the expense, according to Cahill. "Last year our volunteer staff saved the county $616,700. The benefits we receive from our valuable volunteer staff outweigh the cost of the incentive program. Our volunteer staff is priceless."

Source: Kathy Cahill, Volunteer Services Coordinator, Lee County Parks and Recreation, Ft. Myers, FL. Phone (239) 432-2159. E-mail: KCahill@leegov.com

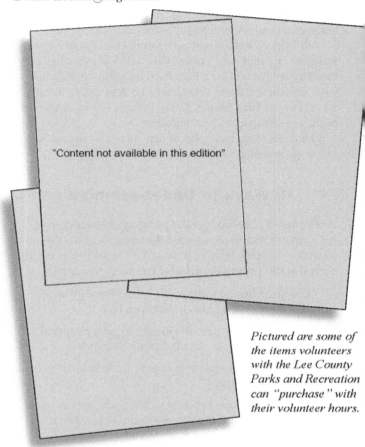

"Content not available in this edition"

Pictured are some of the items volunteers with the Lee County Parks and Recreation can "purchase" with their volunteer hours.

53 What Motivates 'Affiliation-oriented' Volunteers?

Individuals are motivated to volunteer (and keep volunteering) based on what most influences them. For success with *affiliation-oriented volunteers* — those who like being around people:

- Place them in projects in which they work with people.

- Provide a variety of task opportunities that allow them to mix with different volunteer groups.

- Find tasks that require cooperation.

- Provide them with off-task time to interact with coworkers.

- Allow plenty of relationship-building time and activities.

54 Active Listening Tip

When are we least likely to listen to someone? When *we* are doing the talking and the individual chimes in with a comment or thought. That's because we're thinking about what we are saying.

Next time someone comments during your remarks, make a conscious effort to really stop and listen to what's being said. Follow up on what is said: "That's a good point. Tell me more."

You'll have plenty of time later to get back to whatever you were saying at the start of the conversation.

55 Avoid 'Idle Time' By Having Backup Checklist of Tasks

It's not healthy to have volunteers on hand with nothing to do. If they finish a task early, they'll get bored and you'll miss out on getting some tasks accomplished.

Have a prioritized list of secondary projects or tasks available for volunteers if and when they finish a more important job. Having such a list available at all times helps avoid too much down time for these dedicated individuals.

Sample secondary projects list:

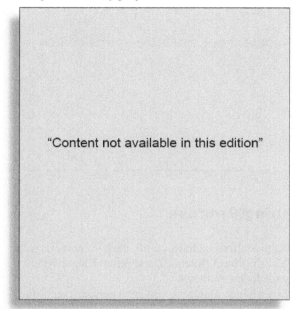

"Content not available in this edition"

57 Survey Former Members

Many member organizations regularly survey members to gather information on current initiatives. Why not survey *former* members to find out how you can improve on your membership benefits and services?

When members decide not to renew their memberships, realize that this is a perfect opportunity to send them a short survey asking why they didn't renew and what they would change, if anything, about the services that were available to them as members.

You could create a simple multiple-choice survey or ask a few questions regarding why they didn't renew and allow members to fill in their thoughts.

Some members may not feel comfortable giving negative feedback, but whatever responses you do receive will hopefully offer insight into why some persons are not continuing their membership with you.

A survey to former members may prove especially helpful during periods of high attrition rates.

56 Advice to Build Long-term Member Loyalty

Does your organization find it difficult to convince members to renew year after year? Take specific actions to build long-term member loyalty. Marilyn Cahill, associate director of membership, California Academy of Sciences (San Francisco, CA), shares various approaches to building long-term member loyalty:

1. **Track the date members joined and print it on their membership card (e.g., "member since 1981").** Reference that date in all correspondence and renewal invoices. If the member joins a new or reopened organization, long-term loyalty can be reinforced with the designation of "Charter or Founding member since 1981."

2. **Designate specific membership length (perhaps 10 years or more) with a special name, (e.g., Centennial Club, Ambassadors or some title relevant to the organization).** These members can be invited to an annual special reception or pre-exhibit opening and thanked for their involvement. A small pin or paperweight can be given to each member as they evolve into the "club."

3. **Create affinity groups to keep members involved.** Through conversations, surveys or self-selection, determine particular areas of interest and target these niches. Form a "modern art guild" or a "friends of the library" group. Encourage involvement of niche membership groups through a newsletter, occasional special lectures or meeting with a curator or senior staff. "Members feel a greater sense of involvement when they receive direct communications from your decision-makers," says Cahill.

Source: Marilyn Cahill, Associate Director of Membership, California Academy of Sciences, San Francisco, CA.
Phone (800) 794-7576. E-mail: mcahill@calacademy.org

58 Offer Special Perks For Those Most Dedicated

How do you distinguish those volunteers who put in extraordinary amounts of time compared to all others? Why not develop a special package of perks for volunteers who meet a milestone number of contributed hours during a specified period of time. For example, you might offer special benefits (on an ongoing basis) to any volunteer who continues to give 60 hours of donated time per month.

What might those special benefits include? Consider:

- Use of a designated lounge
- Special recognition/seating
- Invite to dine with CEO
- Parking privileges
- Staff meeting participation
- Earned sabbatical time
- Inclusion in a prize drawing
- Business cards

59 Mural Celebrates and Motivates Volunteers, Illustrates Hours of Service

What started as a display to showcase volunteers now motivates them as well.

Squam Lakes Natural Science Center (Holderness, NH) prominently displays a large permanent mural dedicated to volunteers in its Trail Head gallery.

The mural, appropriately depicting an outdoor nature scene, is assembled with puzzle pieces bearing volunteer names. The more hours volunteers serve, the more pieces go up on the puzzle; there are spaces for volunteer hours from 200 to 2,000 plus.

Titled "Volunteers Complete the Picture," the mural soon had volunteers asking how many more hours they needed to move up on the puzzle, says Audrey Eisenhauer, volunteer coordinator.

"They'd say, 'how many more hours do I need, a hundred? OK, I can do that in a year'," says Eisenhauer. "It was an unexpected benefit. I certainly didn't plan on it being a motivator" for volunteers to put in more hours.

The mural is updated yearly. Eisenhauer announces which volunteers' pieces will move up at the annual volunteer recognition event and in newsletters.

Source: Audrey Eisenhauer, Volunteer Coordinator, Squam Lakes Natural Science Center, Holderness, NH. Phone (603) 968-7194. E-mail: Audrey.eisenhauer@nhnature.org. Website: www.nhnature.org

"Content not available in this edition"

60 Invite Volunteers Into the Strategic Planning Process

When it's time to create your nonprofit's next five- or 10-year strategic plan, consider involving volunteers.

Volunteer Calgary (Calgary, Alberta, Canada) involved about 100 volunteers during the development of its three-year strategic plan in 2004. "Volunteers are our key stakeholders," says Mario Siciliano, president and CEO. "The idea of locking yourself in a room to create your strategic plan without including your stakeholders didn't make sense to us."

The strategic planning committee involved volunteer board members, community volunteers and volunteers from their nonprofit organizations' membership base. Participants offered their input through focus groups, one-on-one meetings and written and electronic surveys.

"After receiving the written surveys, for example, we held an annual members meeting — involving the 100 volunteers — and asked them specific questions including: What should Volunteer Calgary do in the future? What are some barriers? What are some opportunities?" says Siciliano. "About a year later we held another meeting, presented back to the group and refined their suggestions."

If your organization chooses to involve a large volunteer group, Siciliano recommends setting guidelines.

"Before starting the process, think about how you want to create the plan, present that to the group, get an agreement and then go in that direction," he says. "If you nail that down in the beginning, you can focus on making the plan come together."

Other guidelines include: clarify each volunteer's role; establish clear project timelines; and remove any barriers that may exclude volunteers.

"By involving volunteers, you get a perspective of the individuals you are attempting to serve. It is critically important that those you serve are involved so you have a better understanding of their needs and what they are looking for in services," Siciliano says. "Just like you wouldn't do a strategic plan without staff, I would say you shouldn't do a strategic plan without volunteers. They are an integral part of human resources and ultimately will be the people implementing many components of the plan."

Siciliano says it took a year to complete the strategic plan. "It is worth the extra time to get it on the mark up front. If an organization can do that, it will pay off in the end."

Source: Mario Siciliano, President and CEO, Volunteer Calgary, Calgary, Alberta, Canada. Phone (403) 231-1444. E-mail: msiciliano@volunteercalgary.ab.ca. Website: www.volunteercalgary.ab.ca

61 Take Criticism With Tact

When a volunteer criticizes you, ask how he or she would have handled the situation under similar circumstances. This defuses a potential confrontation and works toward a solution.

62 Retention Tips for Veteran Volunteers

■ To keep your most accomplished volunteers commit-
ted, visit one on one with them and ask what you can
do to make their work more satisfying. Do they need
additional volunteers to assist their efforts? Would they
like to have different hours? Perhaps they want more
leadership responsibilities. Whatever the case, you
won't know how you can help them feel even better
about their work without asking them.

63 Novel (and Free) Volunteer Recognition Idea

Are you looking for a unique — and free — way to recognize volunteers? Enlist the help of area school children.

Ask a preschool or elementary school teacher to have
students draw pictures of people volunteering. On each
picture, have the student (or teacher) write "Thank You."

Present a picture to each volunteer at your next meeting. Or display the artwork throughout the agency.

Added benefit: The students learn more about the value
of volunteers.

64 Motivate Volunteers to Fill Recruitment Needs

Word-of-mouth recruitment is often a core tool for volunteer
managers. Offering incentives for volunteers to recruit
others can make the process more effective.

With a multi-million dollar expansion looming,
volunteer services staff at Randolph Hospital (Asheboro,
NC) knew more volunteers were needed. So Dorothy Lewis,
secretary, came up with "Operation PUSH" as in "Push a
Friend to Volunteer."

Lewis presented the recruitment program plan to
volunteers at a monthly meeting. She gave them push pins
with an "Operation PUSH" label and told them to place
the pin where they could view it daily and think about
volunteers they could recruit.

Lewis also established a set of rules for the volunteers-
recruit-volunteers effort:

• Volunteers were to solicit responsible and dependable
people with a commitment to the role of volunteering.

• The potential candidate had to write down the
volunteer's name on the "referred by" section of the
application.

• Current volunteers were encouraged to invite potential
volunteers to fundraising events and a quick office visit,
possibly with lunch.

• Once a new volunteer was enrolled, the person who
referred him/her should periodically check in to ensure
he/she was handling the tasks involved.

Once a new volunteer had been active for 90 days,
or 50 hours, the "PUSH" volunteer was entitled to a $25
restaurant gift certificate and a new uniform.

Lewis says the prospect of wearing a new uniform
has the most appeal for her volunteers, who now wear an
outdated apricot-colored smock. "PUSH" volunteers who
successfully recruit a new candidate are awarded stylish teal
jackets or golf shirts. Lewis says the new uniforms make the
volunteers who earn them stand out.

"These new uniforms symbolize honor," she says.

"Even our hospital staff ask volunteers why they have
different uniforms."

The program runs Jan. 1 to Dec. 31. Awards are
presented at the annual volunteer awards breakfast held
each April. During the first year of the program, four new
volunteers were recruited from an existing pool of 100, and
two more were lined up after the start of the year.

*Source: Dorothy Lewis, Secretary, Volunteer Services, Randolph
Hospital, Asheboro, NC. Phone (336) 625-5151.
E-mail: dlewis@randolphhospital.org*

"Content not available in this edition"

65 Four Ways to Show You Care

Officials with the Crisis Center (Iowa City, IA) welcome the opportunity to let volunteers know they make a difference.

Patti Fields, director of volunteer services, says with more than 240 volunteers working throughout the Crisis Center, it is important to show appreciation for volunteer contributions.

Fields says appreciation is communicated in four ways:

1. **Staff appreciation.** "It is important volunteers recognize they are appreciated by the entire staff," says Fields. To achieve this, the staff poses for an annual fun photo that centers on the appreciation theme. "One year we wore star-shaped sunglasses for the 'stars in our eyes' theme and another year we wore top hats for our 'hats off to you' theme." Photo placemats are then created and used at the banquet alongside appreciative note cards.

2. **Provide specific information about their impact on the community.** "From the volunteers who sort donations to the volunteers working directly with clients, we make sure they know the work couldn't happen without them," says Fields. "By providing this information, our volunteers feel their work and time impacts the community in which they live."

3. **Peer acknowledgement.** Instead of an ordinary annual awards program, the center decided to let volunteers do the honoring. Fields says awards are given through peer nominations and presented with the specific examples of service honored by the volunteer's peers. "The stories and heartfelt words provided in the nominations cultivate the feeling of community and teamwork within our nonprofit."

4. **Create personal connections.** Fields says letting volunteers know they make a difference can't happen unless you build a relationship with them. By taking the time to get to know them, managers are able to let volunteers know with sincerity and honesty that they make an important difference.

Source: Patti Fields, Director of Volunteer Services, Crisis Center, Iowa City, IA. Phone (319) 351-2726.
E-mail: pfields@jccrisiscenter.org

66 Employ a Volunteer Grievance Procedure

Does your nonprofit have a procedure in place to handle volunteer complaints? Dawn Kasnick, CEO, Girl Scouts of San Gorgonio Council (Redlands, CA), says a volunteer grievance policy is a must-have for volunteer managers.

"You can't expect people to be accountable if you don't tell them what they are accountable for," says Kasnick.

Kasnick recently revised and adopted her agency's grievance policy. The policy, part of the volunteer manual, is shared with volunteers during orientation.

"I want to make our personnel policies very clear to everybody so there are no uncertainties," she says. "This policy gives them a way to get to the bottom of the problem and get an answer."

If a grievance is filed, she says there are four procedural steps they follow:

1. An attempt is made to ascertain all facts and adjust grievances on an informal basis between the volunteer and supervisor.

2. If the volunteer is not satisfied, they have five working days after the grievance presentation to pursue the matter. The grievance is then submitted in writing to the staff person responsible for that functional area. The staff person meets with the volunteer following the receipt of the written grievance and delivers an answer in writing 10 working days after the meeting.

3. If the issue is still unresolved, the aggrieved party may file a written appeal with the grievance committee. The grievance committee — comprised of one staff member, one policy making volunteer (e.g., board member, delegate), one operational volunteer (e.g., troop leader, service area volunteer) and one person selected by the grievant — will meet with the volunteer. They will investigate and deliver an answer to the volunteer.

4. If grievance is still not adjusted, the party may file a written appeal with the CEO. The CEO may meet with the volunteer and, in 10 working days after the meeting and receipt of appeal, deliver his/her answer in writing.

Kasnick says while there is no standard template for a grievance procedure established by the Girl Scouts of the USA, the organization recommends that each council implement its own procedures as part of its volunteer management system.

Kasnick says in the last 10 years she is aware of her council using the grievance policy four times. Two of those times the committee has reversed its decision to remove the volunteer from their position.

Source: Dawn Kasnick, CEO, Girl Scouts of San Gorgonio Council, Redlands, CA. Phone (909) 307-6555.
E-mail: dkasnick@gssgc.org

67 Recognition Ideas for Family Volunteers

It only makes sense that families who volunteer together like to be recognized together. Heather Jack, president, The Volunteer Family (Framingham, MA), offers these ways to recognize families as a whole:

- **Nominate the family for an award.** National awards include the Presidential Volunteer Service Award (www.presidentialserviceawards.gov), the Disney Family Fun Award (www.familyfun.com/volunteers) and the Angel Soft Million Family Service Pledge (www.angelsoft.com/angelsinaction). Many states and cities also have awards.
- **Pitch the story to your local paper** about a family who has really taken an initiative to volunteer for your organization. Have the family sign a photo release.
- **Throw a family volunteer mixer** so family volunteers can meet and mingle with each other.
- **Name something after the family,** such as a tree or flowerbed they planted for your organization.
- **Organize an outing for the family** that appeals to the entire family (e.g., picnic, ball game, pool party, ice cream social or children's theater tickets).
- **Take pictures of each family as they volunteer** and frame them as a gift.
- **Ask families to walk in a parade** on your organization's behalf.
- **Give families a free dinner** at a local family restaurant.

However you choose to recognize your family volunteers, Jack suggests talking to them first to ensure they're okay with it, especially if you're planning to nominate them for awards or telling your local paper about them.

Source: Heather Jack, President, The Volunteer Family, Framingham, MA. Phone (508) 405-2220.
E-mail: hjack@thevolunteerfamily.org

68 Asking Staff to Act Like Mentors to Volunteers

One health system is leading the way when it comes to relationships between staff and volunteers.

Volunteer services departments for the Franciscan Health System hospitals (Tacoma, Federal Way and Lakewood, WA) are creating mentors for volunteers out of staff members in order to provide better communication and connections.

As Sheri Bebbington, volunteer services and Community Health Integration coordinator, says, her job is to coordinate available volunteers with hospital departments needing them.

While Bebbington and fellow Catholic Health Initiatives coordinators still handle the application, screening, orientation and background check processes, department mentors are the ones who interview potential volunteers to make the right fit. Since department staff has firsthand experience as to what their positions entail and they provide training and manage on-site volunteers, Bebbington says it makes sense to give the departments the opportunity to place their own volunteers.

The need for these mentors came from a fast-growing volunteer department that needed to use its resources to the fullest. At first, Bebbington says, they were concerned staff members might feel resentment about having to take on another task, but staff members were happy to do it. By giving staff members the opportunity to choose their volunteers, they are able to cultivate relationships right from the start, creating buy-in for volunteers and staff. Bebbington says this has helped lead to less volunteer turnover.

Bebbington and the other coordinators give the mentors the tools they need to effectively choose and manage their own volunteers. They're given resources and guidelines like a Mentor Connection newsletter, which is sent to mentors and department managers and posted internally on the company website, and a mentor guideline book. In fact, the hospitals are looking into financially rewarding staff members who take on these mentoring roles.

Source: Sheri Bebbington, Coordinator, Volunteer Services, St. Joseph Medical Center, Tacoma, WA.
Phone (253) 426-6785.
E-mail: sheribebbington@fhshealth.org

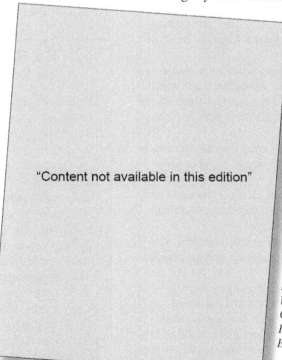

"Content not available in this edition"

69 Avoid Volunteer Burnout

Can you spot volunteer burnout? According to *Hands for Nature: A Volunteer Management Handbook*, developed by Evergreen (Toronto, Ontario, Canada), volunteers who suffer from burnout show a lack of energy, satisfaction, concentration and humor, and decreased self-confidence.

Here are tips to avoid burnout:

1. Make goals realistic, relevant and achievable. Don't make your volunteers reach for an impossible target.

2. Keep the workload manageable.

3. Give your volunteers the opportunity to say no and take breaks.

4. Manage volunteer time efficiently. Since lack of time is one of the greatest barriers to volunteering, make sure the volunteer's workday is planned.

5. Make the volunteer work fun.

— Hands for Nature: A Volunteer Management Handbook, www.evergreen.ca/en/resources/docs/hands/index.html

6. Provide volunteers with a safe and nurturing work environment.

7. Understand who the volunteers are (e.g., personality, availability, skill-set, work interests, etc.) and match the work to the volunteer's skills and interests.

8. Make sure volunteers understand what value their own work adds to the organization's mission.

9. Offer volunteers position variety.

10. Keep communication lines open, allowing volunteers the opportunity to provide feedback.

*— Keith Hocking, Director of
Volunteer-based Programs,
San Francisco AIDS Foundation, San Francisco, CA*

70 Get Your Staff Acquainted With Your Volunteers

Here's a great idea to let your staff and volunteers know what's going on with your volunteer program: Create table tents with a volunteer's picture and biography and place them on tables in your organization's cafeteria or lunchroom.

That's what Lynda Irish did for her volunteers during one Volunteer Week celebration. Irish is director of education and volunteer services at St. Joseph Regional Medical Center (Lewiston, ID).

Each of her 130 volunteers was invited to participate in the table tent display. Irish sent her volunteers a letter and a "get to know you" questionnaire. She also gave them the option of choosing to not participate; however very few choose to opt out.

Irish says the gesture proved a great way to offer much-deserved recognition while also helping staff get to know the volunteers better.

"Very often volunteers come in, do their tasks and don't ever get really acquainted with those they help. And they have very interesting stories," she says.

Staff, visitors and volunteers loved the tents and went from table to table reading the various bios and looking for volunteers they knew personally.

Irish says the tents were a big hit and generally increased awareness about the volunteers and the volunteer program. One volunteer even took her tent to a state volunteer meeting and talked about how much it meant to the volunteers to be publicly recognized and thanked in this manner.

While the table tents are a great idea, Irish does say they are quite an undertaking that requires a great deal of organization and coordination.

Source: Lynda Irish, Director of Education & Volunteer Services, St. Joseph Regional Medical Center, Lewiston, ID. Phone (208) 799-5217. E-mail: lirish@sjrmc.org

71 Be Ready and Willing To Lend a Hand

While there are numerous methods used to motivate volunteers, none are as effective as genuine gestures of help. Although any effort on your part to assist a volunteer with his/her career, personal life or other challenge may be just that — a sincere act of kindness — those caring actions often have a more profound impact on the recipient than any so-called technique you might use to motivate increased service to your organization.

Think of those who have taken the time to personally help you in one way or another and how those actions impacted you. Pretty powerful stuff, isn't it? And while those people who have helped you had no *quid pro quo* in mind, you would no doubt be the first to be there for them if they needed help of some kind.

So as you go about your daily routine, be on the lookout for those who may need a listening ear or a helping hand. Your acts of kindness will bounce back in multiple ways.

72 Ask Your Volunteers for Input

Your volunteers will obviously keep doing what they're doing if they find fulfillment in it. That's why it's important to periodically ask for their input in various ways — one-on-one meetings, surveys, suggestion box, etc.

Answers to these open-end questions will provide you with valuable feedback.

- If you were in charge, how might you change this job?
- How can we show you we care?
- What's most gratifying about what you do here?

- What do you find most challenging about this job (or working here)?
- What would it take to make you feel successful in this job?
- Is there anyone you would like to know about your achievements here?

Most importantly, if you take the time to ask for input, be sure to follow up and inform your volunteers of the ways in which you're following up.

73 Sort Out Volunteers' Goals Before Promoting Them

Have you considered promoting a deserving volunteer in your organization? Vickie Bateman, director, Volunteer Action Center of Bartholomew County (Columbus, IN), says it is important to stay in tune with your volunteers when considering a promotion.

"Recognize where every volunteer is in their quest to reach the goals they have set for themselves and how they are measuring their success," says Bateman.

Within the volunteer pool at the Volunteer Action Center, Bateman says the "Baby Boomers," Gen-Xers and Nexters are individualistic and self-directed.

"They are looking for meaningful work, more influence, more decision-making power and a more active role in designing their work. They are certain to have personal goals in mind when they choose to volunteer. Those goals may include learning a new skill, career exploration or developing a network of influential contacts. A volunteer position that elevates them to a higher level with more responsibility can help them accomplish their goals," says Bateman.

According to Bateman, it is the volunteer manager's responsibility to find out why the volunteer has come to your organization. "This will provide the insight needed to know how to initially place the volunteer and how to plan for promotion, if appropriate."

Bateman recommends discussing with the volunteers:

- Their past experiences.
- Where they see themselves in the future.
- Their definition of success as it relates to volunteering for your organization.
- The steps they will take to measure their own success.

"A promotion doesn't have to be a big jump in responsibility. Some volunteers may only want a small bit of additional responsibility or the trust to make small decisions and the freedom to act upon them. Other volunteers may be eager to take on bigger tasks and welcome the opportunity to show what they are capable of doing and to take credit for their role in the progress of the organization," says Bateman. "It is the volunteer coordinator's role to recognize those volunteers, those opportunities for change and growth and to advocate for the volunteers with their organization administration."

Source: Vickie Bateman, Director, Volunteer Action Agency of Bartholomew County, Columbus, IN. Phone (812) 375-2210. E-mail: vbateman@uwbarthco.org

Volunteer Promotions Equal Retention

Vickie Bateman says promoting a volunteer is a "must" for any volunteer resource manager hoping to retain volunteers.

As a volunteer coordinator of a program that placed volunteers as home visitors with at-risk parents of newborns, Bateman says she had volunteers who were "born to do this work" and who fully understood the challenges parents face.

"Although I was tempted to leave the volunteers in their roles as home visitors, I realized they brought perspective and insight to the program that even the medical and social work professionals supporting the program didn't have," says Bateman. "The best thing I did for the volunteers and the program was to ask these volunteers to take on a new role by joining the team of medical and child development experts who were reviewing and rewriting the parenting curriculum."

After receiving the promotion, volunteers worked with experts to redesign the evaluation methods, rewrite the volunteer training manual and help conduct the volunteer training.

"Successful volunteers stay with your organization. They become the organization's best ambassadors. They become invested in helping the organization and programs grow, and gaining credibility and sustainability in their community," she says.

74 Chapters, Committees Encourage Member Participation and Interaction

Chapters and committees can encourage widespread member involvement in your organization.

The Florida Association of Mortgage Brokers (FAMB) of Tallahassee, FL, is comprised of 14 chapters, with two new chapters being formed, says Frank Cicione, executive director. Members must be affiliated with a chapter.

"Chapters are the lifeblood of our organization," Cicione says.

"Without chapters, the FAMB would be a loose-knit organization of non-interrelated individuals. Each chapter meets regularly, has its own board of directors, officers and bylaws," he says, adding: "Each chapter is self-managing, self-funding and self-budgeting."

Chapter members are actively involved in their communities.

Transcending the organization's stated mission (creating public awareness of a mortgage broker's role), they help raise funds and manpower to assist the community and those in need, says Cicione: "Our members have a heartfelt and vested interest in helping their communities and their neighbors."

Chapters provide future leadership for the state association and help determine its direction. The state association's board of director comprises representatives from each chapter. Directors serve as a direct link between the state association and the individual member.

Committee membership cultivates management and leadership skills required for the state and national level. Only former or current chapter presidents may be appointed to the executive committee of the state association.

Source: Frank Cicione, Executive Director, Florida Association of Mortgage Brokers, Tallahassee, FL. Phone (850) 942-6411. E-mail: frank@famb.org

Committees Enhance Member Communication

The Florida Association of Mortgage Brokers (FAMB) of Tallahassee, FL, comprises numerous committees staffed and chaired by representatives from each chapter. To enhance communication, state committees' members also serve on the corresponding committee in their respective chapter.

FAMB's committees include:

- **Nominating/Past Presidents/Long Range Planning Committees:** Composed of past state-level presidents, the primary responsibility of this committee is to nurture, encourage and select members to serve on the state executive committee. It also provides insight into long-range planning and important current issues.

- **Awards Committee:** Responsible for selecting the winners of the coveted association awards, including large, medium and small Chapter of the Year, State Broker of the Year and State Affiliate Member of the Year, this committee follows strict guidelines, including a regular review of chapters' activities and performance scores.

- **Lenders and Affiliates Committee:** Composed of association members that are not active brokers — including wholesale lenders, appraisers and title companies — this team provides insight and experience on various issues outside of a broker's experience.

- **Political Action Committee (PAC):** Charged with monitoring and approving requests for the association's PAC funds, this group raises funds for PACs by planning and conducting fundraisers.

- **Communications Committee:** This committee encompasses these three key committees: technology, public relations and focus. The technology team improves web-based communications with members, nonmembers and consumers. Public relations members promote the FAMB broker and provides useful consumer information to the public. And the focus committee generates a bi-weekly e-newsletter to more than 20,000 recipients, with information pertinent to the mortgage industry and related industries.

- **Membership and Member Services Committees:** These teams generate ideas to help expand new member growth and keep member retention high. They host a membership booth at various functions, where they distribute literature and provide incentives to join.

- **Convention and Trade Show Committees:** Charged with developing and expanding the theme and activities for the annual convention and trade show, these committees recruit volunteers for the events.

- **Government Affairs Committee:** This committee works with the organization's lobbyist and legal counsel to protect interests of the mortgage industry while still ensuring the needed level of consumer protection within the state. The committee reviews pending legislation on both state and federal levels and brings the findings to the executive committee, board of directors and the chapter members.

- **Bylaws Committee:** This team keeps the state association's bylaws up to date and ensures they accommodate changes needed by the association to run smoothly and efficiently. Its members also review chapter bylaws and provide feedback to the chapters to help ensure bylaws are kept current.

75 Stickers Show Member Support

Officials with Dalton-Whitfield Chamber of Commerce (Dalton, GA) have a clever way of showing members they support them.

Recently the chamber replaced "We appreciate your membership" business cards with "Membership Matters!" stickers.

"'Membership Matters!' stickers are a retention tool used to let chamber members know they are important to us,"  says Beth Morrison, vice president of membership services. "It's a great way to let the store manager know you have been in their business, spending money, doing business and that you recognized and appreciate their membership."

Eight stickers are printed on a business card size sheet of paper, allowing staff, chamber diplomats and executive board members the convenience of carrying several pages of stickers in their wallet in the amount of room they used to keep one business card.

"We would leave the business cards with restaurant checks and it worked when the manager actually saw it. Often the problem was the server would get the card and not pass it on, not understanding the importance of chamber membership," says Morrison.

"This sticker eliminates that problem because it goes directly on credit card receipts that the manager sees when they are processing the day totals. Then when their dues are up for renewal, hopefully they will remember you are doing business with them and sending referrals."

Chamber officials also use the stickers on Christmas cards, invoices, reminder letters and on the back of their own business cards. The cost to produce 2,500 sheets of stickers is $600.

Source: Beth Morrison, Vice President of Membership Services, Dalton-Whitfield Chamber of Commerce, Dalton, GA. Phone (706) 278-7373. E-mail: Morrison@daltonchamber.org

76 Contact Lapsed Volunteers for Quick Recruitment

When you need to fill volunteer positions quickly, consider contacting your inactive volunteers. They've been trained, they know your organization, and visiting with them may help you learn why they left and fix any problems.

Christie Truly, volunteer coordinator, Appalachian Community Hospice (Athens, OH), says that when she came on as volunteer coordinator, she realized the need for more volunteers in areas involving direct patient contact. To get people in fast, she grabbed a list of lapsed volunteers and the phone.

"I introduced myself and got them talking about hospice and why they haven't volunteered for a while," Truly recalls. "I also asked them if they would consider coming back."

Two volunteers came back right away and two more within the month. They received brief refreshers, but many remembered their training on the subjects of grief and death and dying, and were able to step right back in to volunteering.

Interestingly, Truly notes, some of the reasons these persons had quit volunteering resolved on their own and the people just needed someone to reconnect them to the organization. For example, one volunteer had moved, but had since returned to the community. Another person had been dealing with personal issues that resolved before Truly called.

Phoning lapsed donors, Truly was able to learn and address why they had left. Some said they left because they felt there wasn't much for them to do. Truly immediately told them how they were needed and why, (e.g., she wanted to send out more volunteers per week to patients' homes, plus she needed extra hands to cover volunteer sick days).

Other volunteers said they dropped out because of lack of time and not being able to fit volunteer hours into the previous schedule. Truly introduced them to her newly created program that gives fully trained hospice volunteers the opportunity to be "on-call" and come in on nights and weekends.

Source: Christie Truly, Volunteer Coordinator, Appalachian Community Hospice, Athens, OH. Phone (740) 594-8226, ext. 475. E-mail: ctruly@acvna.org

77 An E-newsletter Informs, Involves Members

Try testing an e-newsletter to keep members more informed and involved in your cause. All that's really needed is an e-mail account and a word-processing program. Text can simply be copied and pasted into an e-mail message, then sent to members.

In addition to providing timely news of your organization's programs and upcoming activities that may be of interest to them, the e-newsletter can also serve to solicit member input on any number of topics.

78 Effective Tools for Retaining Members

To retain members, maintain communication, request feedback, encourage participation and give recognition.

Holly Koenig, vice president, Kellen Company (New York, NY), shares how these effective tools can help retain membership:

Communicate — Koenig says to send frequent communications (e.g., press releases, e-mails, etc.), as long as they're pertinent and value-added.

Request Feedback — When a member renews their dues, send an e-mail thanking them and ask for feedback on specific services and current and upcoming projects. By asking for their input, you will ensure their needs are being met.

Engage — Keeping members engaged is vital to retention. Contact new members by phone to personally welcome them. Inquire why the person joined and what their expectations are. Inform them about upcoming activities to get them involved immediately.

Recognize — Recognition of members is equally important. If members don't feel appreciated for a job well done, they may decide to discontinue their membership with your organization. Koenig recommends sending membership participation plaques annually, so if members choose not to renew, the plaques will obviously be absent from their walls.

Source: Holly Koenig, Vice President, Kellen Company, New York, NY. Phone (212) 297-2129. E-mail: hkoenig@kellencompany.com

79 Member Report Card Makes the Grade

A member report card can tell you how your organization is doing.

The Mashantucket Pequot Museum & Research Center (Mashantucket, CT) implemented a member report card a few years ago.

"We wanted to find out how our members felt about their experience," says Denise Braley, membership coordinator. "The survey covered customer service, cost of membership, benefits and interactions with staff."

Members were asked to rate the museum in a variety of areas. The replies are being used to make short- and long-term changes. One immediate change is offering Sunday openings for the temporary gallery, along with a brunch. These openings were previously held on Friday evenings, which wasn't convenient for many members. Braley says this has increased turnout.

The report card form was a self-mailer to be returned directly to the executive director, who read all of the responses before the membership department. The report card was mailed with every member's renewal notice monthly for a year. Postage was paid by the museum.

"We felt this would be a good sampling of time and responses," Braley says. "We sent out 3,000 report cards and our return was 310. Some of our members did not answer all questions and some cards were left blank."

The responses were entered into an Excel spreadsheet. Charts were made to show the progress. This report was then sent to all levels of management for their review.

"The form has been a wonderful tool to gather information," Braley says. "We will use it again once some of our new members have been with us for a year or so."

Source: Denise Braley, Membership Coordinator, Mashantucket Pequot Museum & Research Center, Mashantucket, CT. Phone (860) 396-6890. E-mail: dbraley@mptn-nsn.gov

"Content not available in this edition"

80 Offer Training for High Stress Positions

"Taking Care of Ourselves" is the motto and the title of a special training session for volunteers at the Women's Resource Center of the NRV (Radford, VA).

Volunteers at the Women's Resource Center work directly with victims of domestic violence and sexual assault, putting them at high risk for burnout and compassion fatigue.

Over the years, two seasoned volunteers, Eliott Chamberlin-Long and Kathryn Ryder, used their experience and developed materials and content for combating stress. "Taking Care of Ourselves" touches on: healthy habits, stress relievers and emotional health. "We asked participants to reflect on quotes about boundaries and list examples of how stress and vicarious traumatization (compassion fatigue) manifest within them and also ways they currently manage it," say Chamberlin-Long and Ryder.

- **Healthy Habits** — There is information on the handouts about overall health, as well as ways to prevent stress from taking too great of a toll. Exercise, eating well and getting enough sleep are highlighted.

- **Stress Relievers** — Handouts list ideas, and the trainers demonstrate several techniques, such as breathing meditation, which can be done anywhere, anytime. They also demonstrate progressive muscle relaxation and imagery.

- **Emotional Health** — During the section on boundaries, the focus is directly on emotional health, learning to say no and developing a safe and healthy "filter" for things they let in and keep out of our lives. When they talk about secondary traumatization, they point out how hearing others' stories can affect emotional health by changing the way they think about the world. During the brainstorming of stress-reduction ideas, participants often touch on strategies for emotional release in the way of journaling, talking to friends, or taking a break from stressful situations.

"When people deal with crisis on a regular basis, there are bound to be some negative results. This presentation is intended to 'head it off at the pass.' We cannot run our program effectively if we don't allow our volunteers the time and space to take care of themselves and give them permission to work out their issues," says Mary Forti, volunteer coordinator.

Source: Eliott Chamberlin-Long and Kathryn Ryder, Volunteers, Mary Forti, Volunteer Coordinator, Women's Resource Center, Radford, VA. Phone (540) 639-1123. E-mail: volunteers@wrcnrv.org

Stress Relief Through Relaxation

1. **Deep Breathing** — Breathe in deeply through the nose, letting your stomach expand as much as possible. Once you have breathed in as much as possible, hold your breath for a few seconds and then exhale slowly through your mouth. Repeat three to four times several times a day.

2. **Active Relaxation** — Tense then relax each muscle of the body. Start with the muscles in your head and move down to your feet.

3. **Stretching Exercises** — By sitting or standing at your workstation you can stretch your shoulders, arms, back, sides, neck, wrists, hands and forearms. To stretch your hands spread out your fingers until you feel a gentle stretch, relax and close. Repeat 10 to 15 times per hand.

4. **Visualization** — Visualize a successful outcome to a stressful situation. Or visualize a peaceful scene, such as ocean waves lapping on a beach to create relaxation.

5. **Passive Relaxation** — Meditate once or twice a day for 10 to 20 minutes in a quiet place while concentrating on a point of focus, having a passive accepting attitude and a comfortable position.

6. **Yoga** — Slow, deliberate postures with carefully controlled breathing.

7. **Biofeedback** — Send direct messages to various parts of the body to get a desired response. For example, people have been able to prevent frostbite by sending a message to their hands to stay warm. Also used to control chronic pain.

What Volunteers Said About the Training

Things I liked:
- Demonstration of relaxation techniques.
- Exercises.
- Great interactions and demonstration.
- Breathing exercises.
- I really liked the responsible to/responsible for distinction. And I always like a chance to breathe.
- The meditation exercise and stress preventing tips.
- Relaxation techniques.

- I liked that the speakers gave us ideas about how to take care of ourselves emotionally and physically. I think these will be much needed and used.
- Quotes. Breathing.
- Pie. Quotes.
- Laying on the floor.
- Loved the meditation. Liked the stress busters. Elliot/Kathryn are awesome.
- Learning stress. Relaxation techniques.

81 Create a Mentoring Program

The National Press Photographers Association (NPPA) in Golden Valley, MN launched its online-based mentoring program as a way to re-engage its older members, many of whom were no longer interested in participating in the association's educational programs or photo competitions, says Ron Stover, the program's chair.

Any current member can use NPPA's online mentoring program database to locate and establish a mentoring relationship. The database lists mentors by their craft (still or video) and provides basic information, a short bio, a list of specialties and contact information. Mentors and mentees can communicate via e-mail, phone and mail.

The idea behind the program, says Stover, is that the mentor is someone the member can talk to about, for example, how to best handle a story or how to deal with an unfamiliar professional issue.

Because the program is online-based and mentees contact mentors directly, he says, it has been hard to track its success. "We do know that it is one of the most hit-upon sections of our website." One way they attempt to track the success is through an annual survey of mentors, says Stover. "We ask them how many people they are currently seeing and whether they still want to be on the list. Of those who respond to the survey, half say they are being contacted and mentoring to some degree."

Stover says they designed the program to be user-friendly and free. Two volunteer mentoring program chairs keep track of it and their contact information is on the website for questions or assistance. In the beginning, the site listed all mentors nationwide and members found that overwhelming, he says. "The mentor database is now divided into regions so when a member signs in, their information is cross-checked to the database, bringing up mentors from their particular region."

They kickstarted the program by contacting the association's core members to see which of them might be interested in mentoring. "We started with 25 mentors," Stover says. "We also did an article about it in our national magazine and followed up with ads and mentioned it in our regional e-mail newsletter. Within six months we had 50 to 60 mentors." The program currently has about 80 mentors.

The hardest part of the program is getting mentees engaged, says Stover. "We have many mentors who have never been contacted. Others are contacted once or twice and then they never hear from the mentee again."

For more info visit NPPA's website (www.nppa.org/professional_development/mentoring/).

Source: Ron Stover, Chair, National Mentoring Program, National Press Photographers Association, Golden Valley, MN. Phone (612) 685-0907. E-mail: ronstover@comcast.net

82 Encourage Automatic Renewals With Member Savings

Do you offer your members a yearly "automatic renewal" option?

If not, consider doing so. You may find it will increase your renewal response rate.

To motivate more members to sign up for automatic renewal, offer a price break for anyone who agrees to the automatic renewal alternative.

This chart gives you a template from which to work to create a format for your organization's member renewal rates.

Membership Level		
Senior/student	$15 ❑	
Individual	$35 ❑	
Family	$50 ❑	$45* ❑
Donor	$125 ❑	$112* ❑
Charter	$250 ❑	$225* ❑
Leader	$500 ❑	$450* ❑
Director	$1,000 ❑	$900* ❑
Automatic Renewal *		

83 Honor Your Volunteers' Psychological Contract

Did you know that the minute a new volunteer walks through your door, his or her motivation for being there changes? While the person may have been motivated to volunteer for your organization because of altruistic reasons, such as wanting to give back to the community, his or her motivation for *staying* is based on something much more practical.

When an individual accepts a volunteer position with your organization, a "psychological contract" is formed. This contract consists of a set of expectations held by both the individual and the organization. If you fail to meet the volunteer's expectations, chances are, her or she will leave and never come back.

That's why you need to spend time during the interview process to develop a clear and concise psychological contract. Encourage volunteers to be explicit about their contract, what they expect to give and what they expect from their work. Only when you know this can you develop meaningful volunteer projects for people. But remember — this contract also gives volunteers the right *not* to do something.

84 Involve Members to Retain Them

The most successful nonprofits have similar retention strategies as traditional, mainly financially driven organizations, says Patti Fralix, president, The Fralix Group Inc. (Raleigh, NC), a corporate management and communications consultant firm.

"Nonprofits have a mission that is often at least as important as other variables to members and employees," Fralix says. "We shouldn't assume, however, nonprofits don't need to utilize the same retention strategies as for-profits."

Generational differences often affect which retention strategies are most effective. Younger workers, for example, are often as motivated by non-monetary variables as by monetary.

"Don't misinterpret this; money does matter," Fralix says. "However, younger workers are often motivated by challenge, being included in project work in which they can see their involvement in the end result and other growth opportunities."

Nonprofits can "inspire positive change" with members and employees by making sure they're in touch with both groups.

"In other words, when we feel included, involved and that our ideas are important to an organization as a whole, that stimulates our passion in ways that directly affect the success of the organization," Fralix says.

Source: Patti Fralix, President, The Fralix Group Inc., Raleigh, NC. Phone (919) 847-3440. E-mail: pfralix@fralixgroup.com

85 Let Volunteers Get to Know You

Do your volunteers feel you are accessible? In what ways can they contact you?

Volunteers' enthusiasm can be tied to their level of connectivity to you, their supervisor. If they sense you're inaccessible, their interest may wane. If they are able to connect with you in various ways, they'll feel more a part of your team.

To help your volunteers feel you are accessible:

* **Ask them for input on their current projects.** What's working? What's not? How would they do it differently next time?

* **Communicate in various ways.** E-mail individual messages. Hold group meetings with volunteers who are working on the same projects. Make unscheduled visits while they work.
* **Show your personal side.** Host socials away from your workplace. Take an interest in volunteers' personal lives.

Recognize that your volunteers seek support and affirmation from you. Understand how they want to be connected to the one who's leading their efforts.

86 Seven Ways to Cater to 'Senior' Volunteers

Senior citizens are often times among the most sought-after volunteers. They have available time — even during workday hours. They are dependable. And they find gratification in doing good deeds.

So what can you do to attract and retain senior citizens? Each of these ideas caters to this special group:

1. **Build flex time into seniors' tasks.** Make it clear that these folks can give as little as an hour a week or far more time.

2. **Offer pick-up and delivery services.** There may be those who would love to give of their time but either don't drive or are reluctant to fight traffic.

3. **Give thought to the assignments you make.** Prepare an offering of tasks from which seniors can choose — those that take into consideration their physical limitations.

4. **Mix in some fun that caters to the 60-plus crowd.** Play some background music from the swing band era. Prepare and serve a "retro" lunch from the '60s. Offer a series of speakers during non-work hours who will present topics of interest to this group: Reflections on WWII, the history of quilt making, travelogues, estate planning and more.

5. **Provide a comfortable work environment.** Offer adequate lighting, comfortable seating, minimal noise, pleasant room temperature, etc.

6. **Incorporate time to socialize.** Most seniors are energized by the chance to visit with their peers. Offer some fun opportunities, both during and outside of normal work hours, especially tailored to this group.

7. **Say "thank you" in ways that are special to seniors.** Pay a personal visit to a senior's home for no reason other than to chat. Offer health- or meal-related discounts or freebies. Take a moment to celebrate individual birthdays. Hold drawings for donated items.

87 Make a Good First Impression Among New Volunteers

First impressions are vitally important in getting a volunteer relationship off to a good start. These actions on your part will help to ensure a positive beginning:

Give all employees a "heads up" for the volunteer's first day — Make them aware of the new volunteer's name, and encourage them to welcome him/her. A greeting from a receptionist such as "Welcome, [Name]. So glad you're here!" will go a long way in making that good first impression.

Don't delay an orientation and tour — Show each new volunteer around as soon as he/she arrives. Start with the workplace but include the amenities such as restrooms and coffee machine to help them feel comfortable in their new surroundings.

Have work ready — Having something ready for the volunteer to do will make him/her feel wanted. Conversely, if the volunteer has to wait while you "find something for them to do," this may leave him/her feeling more like the proverbial "third wheel."

88 Member Survey Provides Museum Direction

Are you looking for a tool that provides a reliable source of member information including rationale for joining, opinions about the organization and their relationship to the larger community? Consider conducting a member survey.

Jennifer Thomas, membership director, Saint Louis Art Museum (St. Louis, MO) talks about their decision to survey the museum's members:

Why did you conduct a member survey?
"There were four main reasons: 1) the last survey was more than 10 years ago; 2) a recent rate increase and level restructuring; 3) an upcoming capital expansion; and 4) exhibition schedule."

How many members (current and lapsed) received the survey?
"Last May, 2,000 current members and 2,500 lapsed members received the survey, a cover letter and a museum magnet, through the mail."

What was the percentage of members (current and lapsed) who responded?
"30 percent of current members and 10 percent of lapsed members responded within the requested time period (six weeks)."

What did you learn from the survey?
" From our survey, we developed a profile of our current members; learned our members most value free exhibition admission; confirmed the exhibition schedule is one of the most important factors they consider when joining and visiting; learned our members are very satisfied with our benefits package; learned our lapsed members and current members differ in some key ways (lapsed members are younger and have children in the household and are more value-driven and less philanthropically motivated than current members); and learned our members are hungry for e-mail communication and event reminders."

What follow up was taken because of the survey?
"After the membership department viewed the survey it was distributed to key staff in various departments. Since that time, we have bolstered our onsite sales efforts to capture more new members, created new onsite sales materials to help patrons understand the true value of membership and changed the way we talk to our lapsed member in solicitations to reflect the younger audience and their desire to see special exhibitions."

Source: Jennifer Thomas, Membership Director, Saint Louis Art Museum, St. Louis, MO. Phone (314) 655-5385. E-mail: jennifer.thomas@ slam.org

"Content not available in this edition"

"Content not available in this edition"

89   Put the Kibosh on Gossip

What can you do to eliminate, or at least diminish, volunteer gossip in your organization?

Beth Bloomfield, director, retired and senior volunteer program, Volunteer Center Orange County (Santa Ana, CA), says a written gossip policy should be mandatory.

"A written policy should lay out a definition of gossip and the consequences of gossiping," says Bloomfield. "The policy may be created by your board of directors, senior staff, HR department or a volunteer manager may even wish to create the policy in partnership with their volunteers."

Bloomfield says avoiding the problem because a volunteer manager is unprepared and uncomfortable addressing gossip may be harmful. "Gossip can undermine morale, affect productivity and sometimes even lead to the loss of volunteers. If volunteers are not taught by their supervisor to effectively handle gossip, it could affect a volunteer's creativity and commitment to the organization they serve."

Rumors, Griping and Gossip

What is the distinction among rumors, griping and gossip? Bloomfield says each has a different definition and resolution.

- **Rumors** are about imminent organizational or team issues, such as pending reorganization, staff departures or funding challenges. "The best way to deal with rumors is to keep your volunteers informed about issues that affect them," she says.

- **Griping** is a response to some concrete issue that irritates a volunteer. "The best way to deal with griping is to listen and explore options to remove any real obstacles that are getting between your volunteers and their goals."

- **Gossip** always deals with a topic that doesn't directly affect the people doing the gossiping. It's either about what they heard someone say to somebody else, or even worse, it's about personal affairs of other volunteers or staff members. "The only way to deal with gossip is to check it the moment it comes to your attention and encourage and train the organization's volunteers and staff to do the same," says Bloomfield.

Bloomfield offers these tips when dealing with gossip among volunteers:

1. **Don't gossip yourself.**
2. **Curb others who gossip and promote peer responsibility to do the same.**
3. **Decide how you will address gossip.** During a training exercise practice these responses one may ask the gossiper: Is this confidential? Why do I need to know this? If you were (Name) would you want us discussing this? After creating a good list of responses, give volunteers the opportunity to role-play and practice their skill.
4. **Make a distinction between rumors, griping and gossip.** Bloomfield offers this exercise: First give the definitions, then place rumors, griping and gossip examples on index cards. Place the cards in a container and let each participant choose a card. Divide into small groups and have each group decide: 1) Is the statement rumor, gripe or gossip? 2) If you were the subject of the statement, would you want this being discussed? 3) What are the possible intents of the person who shared this information? and 4) How would you recommend someone deal with this?
5. **Consider why someone is gossiping and learn from it.** Are volunteers bored and filling up their time with gossip? Are they gossiping as a way to establish friendship? When you understand why someone is a gossiper, then you have valuable information on how to better change their behavior.
6. **Call in expert help when necessary.** If gossip has become gospel, you may want to ask for assistance.
7. **Change gossip content.** Consider having encouraging "gossip for good" — focusing on others' successes and good news.

Source: Beth Bloomfield, Director, Retired and Senior Volunteer Program, Volunteer Center Orange County, Santa Ana, CA. Phone (714) 953-5757, ext. 115. E-mail: bbloomfield@volunteercenter.org

Practice the Four-way Test

When confronted by gossip, volunteers should practice the Four-way Test.

The test involves volunteers asking themselves four questions before they speak:

1. Is it the truth?
2. Is it fair to all concerned?
3. Will it build good will and better friendship?
4. Will it be beneficial to all concerned?

"If anyone in our presence engages in gossip that does not pass the Four-way Test, we will gently and firmly address the gossiper at that moment," says Bloomfield.

90 Should You Provide Members Lapel Pins?

Lapel pins. They're simple, inexpensive for the most part and help build pride among members. So why not offer them to your members?

Members who wear their pins obviously take pride in being associated with your cause. Equally important, nonmembers see the pins and ask questions that may lead to them becoming members.

In addition to building member loyalty and attracting the interest of nonmembers, pins make great ways to recognize members in many ways (e.g., length of service, achievements, financial contribution levels, etc.). An organization may offer different pins for different reasons. Some organizations award pins based on member-recruit-member campaigns.

If cost is preventing you from providing members with pins, find a donor or sponsor who will underwrite the cost of purchasing them. Or, perhaps you will want to award some pins and sell others as a revenue source.

Organizations That Offer Pins

Here's a small sampling of member organizations that either provide or sell pins to their members:

Brodhead, WI Chamber of Commerce
(www.brodheadchamber.org)

Cheetah Conservation Fund
(www.cheetah.org/?nd=member)

Michigan State University
(www.msualum.com/secure/life-mbrs)

Where to Go for Lapel Pins

Lapel Pins R Us (www.lapelpinsrus.com)

Lapel Pin Superstore (www.lapelpinsuperstore.com)

PinSource (www.pinsource.com)

Quality Lapel Pins (www.qualitylapelpins.com)

---

91 Five Ways to Recognize High School Volunteers

If you rely on high-school-aged volunteers, you know that the ways used to recognize and affirm them are different from methods you may use with other volunteers. They're a group that requires special types of recognition.

Use any of these methods to pat your high school volunteers on the back:

1. Find out when all-school assemblies are scheduled and get permission to make a special award just prior to the main event — while you have a captive audience.

2. Do a brief "kudos" article for the school newspaper or newsletter that praises your high school volunteers. Your students will love being recognized among their peers.

3. Write an unsolicited letter of reference — To Whom It May Concern — delineating a student volunteer's accomplishments. Give it to the student to use for landing a summer job or to include with college entrance materials.

4. Write a letter of commendation to the parents of the student volunteer praising his/her values and work ethic. What better reward could a parent ask for than to have a child praised for a job well done? Chances are the student won't mind hearing about the letter as well.

5. Identify various student awards/recognition given throughout your community — mayor's youth commission, student of the month, etc. — and nominate your top student volunteers for the honor.

---

92 Show Volunteers They Are Part of Your Team

Treating volunteers with the respect and professionalism they deserve will help keep them invested in your cause.

To let her volunteers know they are as important as paid staff, Lakeesha Campbell, volunteer coordinator, Presbyterian Hospice and Palliative Care (Charlotte, NC), holds *monthly volunteer planning meetings* similar to those offered to paid staff.

All volunteers are invited to the hour-long meetings held the fourth Monday of each month. Campbell uses the meetings for a variety of purposes such as education, in-services and as a social outlet for volunteers. Topics, based on volunteer feedback, include: "Appropriate Boundaries When Volunteering with Patients," "Advanced Directives," "Diversity Among Religions" and "Annual Mandatory Education."

Campbell says the meetings keep her organized and involved with volunteers while providing an excellent way for volunteers to build relationships with each other.

Source: Lakeesha Campbell, Volunteer Coordinator, Presbyterian Hospice and Palliative Care, Charlotte, NC. Phone (704) 384-3527. E-mail: lcampbell@novanthealth.org

93 Consider Out-of-the-ordinary Field Trips for Volunteers

Remember school field trips? You were so excited you couldn't sleep the night before! Something new. Something fun. A day away from the normal routine — with friends!

Field trips don't have to be just for students. They can be a great way to encourage friendship and fellowship in your volunteers while also providing a fun and possibly educational adventure. Here are five reasons to invest time in field trips:

1. **A way to say thanks.** Field trips offer an additional way to reward volunteers for their gift of time to your organization and those you serve.

2. **A means to attract new volunteers.** Being able to tell would-be volunteers about some of your recent field trips could help with recruitment efforts.

3. **An opportunity to learn.** Some field trips may serve as educational opportunities for volunteers that may, in fact, benefit your organization in return.

4. **A chance to sing your praises.** Your volunteers will spread good news about your organization as they tell friends, families and acquaintances of their adventure.

5. **A tactic to inspire volunteers.** Off-site adventures will energize your volunteers and reinforce their loyalty to your organization.

Consider offering quarterly or even monthly field trips for some or all of your volunteers. Explore field trip possibilities that may provide beyond-the-norm experiences. For example, if your organization has a major corporate partner, consider a visit to that corporate location where your volunteers can enjoy a tour and meet with a select group of the corporation's employees. See additional trip ideas, below.

Field Trip Ideas to Recharge, Reward, Inspire Volunteers

Here are volunteer field trip ideas to get you started:

- Tour another agency with a connection to your mission or services.

- Arrange a trip to one of your satellite locations. Have persons who benefit from or witness benefits of your organization share their stories.

- Secure donated tickets to a sporting event, complete with a tailgate party. Have your group recognized on the loudspeaker or scoreboard.

- Take a bus to meet with your chapters throughout the state or region. Come prepared to share volunteer success stories, and have them do the same.

- Exchange field trip hosting duties with another non-profit organization.

- Tour a business or other entity with a connection to your organization (e.g., take library volunteers to a book bindery or printer; church volunteers to a bible camp; humane society volunteers to the zoo).

- Relive field trip memories of school days in just-for-fun outings to museums, cultural sites or theatres.

- Indulge volunteers with a brunch trip to a bed-and-breakfast, day trip to an arts/crafts or renaissance fair or worry-free day of shopping.

---

94 Expand Online Member Benefits

How often do you evaluate the member benefits you offer?

Increasing numbers of organizations are offering online member perks as part of their total benefits program. Here's a small sampling of online benefits to consider:

- Screensavers — Provide access to several different screensavers with images related to your organization's mission and programs.
- Education, training, certification opportunities — Make e-learning available.
- Online store — Offer gift items at a member discount that can only be purchased online.
- Audio features — Give members-only audio tours or special podcasts of interest.
- Access to online publications — Provide members exclusive "insider" news and opinions.
- Links to members' sites — Allow website visitors to connect to members' professional or personal websites.
- Special e-mail address — Offer a members-only e-mail alias (JohnDoe@yourdomain.org).
- Networking — Allow members to network with one another via a member directory, bulletin boards, listservs, chatrooms and more.
- Job opportunities — Provide members the opportunity to list and search job openings via your website.

95 Prepare Exit Interview Questions With Thought

Do you conduct exit interviews when volunteers leave your service? Their answers can provide a valuable insight into improvements that need to be made, particularly those that relate to volunteers' duties.

A consistent list of exit interview questions will help you to identify areas that may need to be addressed. These sample questions will help you come up with a list that best fits your needs:

1. What did you like best about your job here? What did you dislike most?

2. Why are you choosing to leave at this time?

3. What would need to change here in order for you to reverse your decision about leaving?

4. How would you rewrite your position description?

5. What will you take from this experience that you could apply elsewhere?

In addition to helping you make improvements, this exit interview process shows respect for those leaving and makes for a more positive impression.

96 Spotlight Offers Recognition, Recruitment, Motivation

It's a slam-dunk when you can not only recognize outstanding volunteers, but also motivate other volunteers and recruit new ones. Birth To Three's (Eugene, OR) website does just that with its quarterly volunteer spotlight.

"It makes the volunteer feel special and appreciated," says Sarah Bachhuber Peroutka, community relations specialist. "It lets others know we notice, appreciate and are proud of our volunteers."

View the volunteer spotlight page at www.birthto3.org and select "spotlights" under the volunteer tab. The website address is put on all Birth To Three's printed materials, along with periodic mentions in newsletters.

"I hope anyone who reads them would react by thinking,

'I could do that!' or 'Their volunteers really love what they do, Birth To Three must be a great place!'" says Peroutka.

Peroutka chooses which volunteers to spotlight. "I pick people who I consider inspirational and interesting and hope to convey that we have a richly diverse group of volunteers."

After selecting a volunteer to feature, she provides the questions and lets them review what she's written before posting it. Peroutka also asks volunteers to supply a picture to go along with the spotlight. If the person is a minor, Peroutka gets permission from their parents.

Source: Sarah Bachhuber Peroutka, Community Relations Specialist, Birth To Three, Eugene, OR. Phone (541) 349-7793. E-mail: sarahp@birthto3.org

97 Nurturing Helps Volunteer Retention Efforts

Volunteer nurturing plays a critical role in retention.

Kristie Fiegen, president, Junior Achievement of South Dakota (Sioux Falls, SD), says their nurturing efforts have earned their program the highest volunteer retention rate among Junior Achievement programs in the U.S.

"The quality of our volunteer consultants is the quality of our program," says Fiegen.

To build a great program, Fiegen only accepts volunteers referred by other volunteers or board members. Once recruited, volunteers attend detailed training sessions facilitated by seasoned consultants and learn their roles and program expectations.

As they prepare for their classroom visits, new consultants may need additional support. Volunteer liaisons, trained consultants themselves, maintain regular contact with first-time consultants and mentor them through any challenges. Fiegen feels the mentoring component of volunteer nurturing is crucial to their comfort level and

retention. During the busy season, Junior Achievement staff correspond with liaisons who monitor their consultants to determine if anyone has become overwhelmed or experienced a life change that has lowered their ability to deliver a quality program. According to Fiegen, "Good organizations also train alternates who can be quickly contacted to fill in for volunteers when things come up, which they often do."

To keep new and returning volunteers energized, Junior Achievement employees work with teachers to request that students write personal thank-you cards to their consultants. At the end of the school year, volunteers are invited to recognition events that reiterate the organization's mission and how important volunteers are in the lives of South Dakota children.

Source: Kristie Fiegen, President, Junior Achievement of South Dakota, Sioux Falls, SD. Phone (605) 336-7318. E-mail: jasd@jasd.org

98 | Large Awards Program Generates Big Benefits

A large awards program involves a lot of hard work, but can generate motivation and enthusiasm for your membership throughout the year.

The Pinnacle Awards is an extensive program created by the Jackson Area Chamber of Commerce (Jackson, TN). For 21 years, the program has promoted the excellence of the business membership and recognized those who have risen to the "pinnacle" of leadership.

The program has many parts that add to its success:

The Application Process — "There is an eight-page application that a company must complete and provide supporting data," says Lisa Webb, manager of membership development.

Areas addressed in the application include: history/growth; customer service excellence; employee satisfaction; and community involvement.

An out-of-town panel of judges selects the winners to ensure decisions are fair and unbiased. The community involvement section is judged by local business leaders, who can verify the applicant is meeting the community needs through service work.

Press Conference — The chamber holds a press conference the Friday before the gala. "All nominees/applicants are recognized, as well as sponsors, and the media has a chance to interact with the applicants," Webb says.

Awards Luncheon — The Emerging Business Awards Luncheon is held the same week as the Pinnacle Awards Gala to recognize growing businesses. The emerging winners are again recognized at the gala. Award applicants have a chance to support and to network with another.

Program Brochure — The glossy, magazine-style awards brochure features a photo and information about the applicants.

"It's a chance for more publicity," Webb says. "The booklets have become one thing everyone looks forward to and keeps. It allows businesses to showcase themselves to our audience of about 400. It also helps applicants feel like they are involved in the evening, even if they don't win. It's another one of those 'feel good' things about the evening."

Pre-event Party — "Before the gala, we hold an invitation-only champagne reception for applicants and sponsors," Webb says. "It makes the evening a little more special."

The Gala Event — The Pinnacle Awards Gala includes a catered dinner, open wine bar and a special ceremony.

Nominees have short videos produced and when the winner is announced, their clip is played. Award recipients receive a beautiful crystal and marble award, symbolizing enterprise and excellence.

TV Coverage — The gala event is taped for TV coverage and televised on a local station for weeks following the ceremony. Winners receive a DVD copy of the evening.

"The television coverage gives applicants good PR," Webb says. "Also, the community loves to watch the replay — we get many calls about the schedule."

The chamber doesn't have an agreement with the local station, but they receive a small discount on services since they're an event sponsor. The chamber covers the costs of applicant videos, equipment at the event and the TV spots out of the sponsorship dollars raised for the awards program.

Source: Lisa Webb, Manager, Membership Development, Jackson Area Chamber of Commerce, Jackson, TN. Phone (731) 423-2200. E-mail: lwebb@jacksontn.com

---

Handbook Enhances Member Involvement

Information about the chamber's Pinnacle Awards can be found in its handbook, *Making the Most of Your Membership — A Handbook for All Chamber Members.*

"We give this to new members in their membership packet and to existing members in our orientation sessions to let folks see what we have to offer," says Webb. "Sometimes people just want a hard copy of our services so they can read it to see how they can fit into our services and programs."

Webb writes and edits the handbook but staff members give their input as well. The handbook is updated annually. The 35-page publication includes the following sections:

- New Member Benefits
- Member Benefits
- Networking Opportunities
- Marketing Opportunities and Sponsorships
- Training and Resource Programs
- Leadership Programs
- Awards Events
- Involvement Opportunities
- Chamber Contact Data
- Staff Directory

The handbook is free and some information can be found on the chamber's website.

"The benefit is when I talk to a business about joining the chamber, I can pull that book out and go through it with them, face to face," Webb says. "The Internet is a great tool, but you can't beat one-on-one interaction."

99 Tactics to Retain Members

How do you develop fresh, new ideas to retain members?

Cindy Haimowitz, member manager, Security Industry Association (Alexandria, VA), identifies three tactics that led to an 85 percent retention rate last year:

1. **Distribute a weekly membership report.** Staff receives a list of people who have and haven't renewed their memberships. "It's important to keep staff involved," she says. "The more people involved on the recruiting team, the better. It's everybody's job to keep those members."

2. **Involve board members.** Board members also receive a list and are asked to personally contact those members who haven't renewed. "Who better than board members to show others the value of membership?"

3. **Include a monthly e-newsletter reminder.** An "in your face" message was created to remind members to renew. On the front of the bi-weekly e-newsletter, a friendly reminder is strategically placed to remind members to renew. "After the e-newsletter is released, I receive a series of phone calls and e-mails regarding membership and we also see a jump in renewals," Haimowitz says.

Source: Cindy Haimowitz, Member Manager, Security Industry Association, Alexandria, VA. Phone (703) 647-8488. E-mail: chaimowitz@siaonline.org

100 Give Your Volunteers Reasons to Stick Around

Does your organization have the reputation of being a place where people come in, do a little bit of time and go on their way?

To encourage volunteers to stay put, consider implementing one or all of the following ideas:

▶ **A "new-recruit" training program** — Appoint a "buddy" for new volunteers — to not only teach them things like where the time sheets are located, but to also help them socialize, join them for lunch and introduce them around.

▶ **A "coffee klatch" program** — Appoint a time when volunteers can mix and mingle with paid staff or board members in an unstructured, casual setting. This type of session can help volunteers feel valued and involved in the organization, and allows them to speak freely about what's on their mind.

▶ **Better supervisory training** — Provide formal training for paid staff. Make sure your volunteer manager and key staff members have the leadership and technical skills necessary to direct volunteers.

101 Nurture 'Achievement' To Motivate Volunteers

Who among your existing volunteers is energized by making achievements? By identifying those individuals, you can motivate them by:

- Offering feedback
- Incorporating competition
- Providing responsibility
- Furnishing goals
- Sharing problems that they will perceive as challenges
- Providing quantifiable parameters allowing them to measure their success
- Sharing past achievements that existing volunteers can work to surpass

102 Occasionally Visit Your Facility During 'Off Hours'

Do you have volunteers who work the night shift or during "off hours" at your organization? If so, you might want to pay spot visits to your facility during those times. Occasionally it's a good idea to drop by unexpectedly. There's nothing like a periodic visit to let those volunteers know you care about both them and the organization all of the time.

103 Keep Former Chairpersons Involved

It's quite probable you have projects that are headed by a new chairperson each year. Rather than "retiring" those chairs, why not create an exclusive club that includes all former chairpersons?

Assemble the group at least once a year for a get-together and put them in charge with some ongoing responsibility that keeps them involved with your volunteer activities.

104 Explore New Types of Member Benefits

What types of benefits do you currently offer your members? Meet with staff and key members to analyze those benefits and create a list of additional options that may be cost effective and attractive to members.

Member benefits worth exploring:

- ❏ Free/discounted event admittance
- ❏ Insurance
- ❏ Web hosting, design
- ❏ Availability of mailing lists
- ❏ Interest group opportunities
- ❏ Discounts on purchases of supplies, gifts, services and other items
- ❏ Membership directory

- ❏ Members-only social gatherings or educational opportunities
- ❏ Legal services
- ❏ Special types of recognition
- ❏ Insider information
- ❏ Access to restricted website pages
- ❏ Travel: field trips and tours
- ❏ Special publications
- ❏ Reciprocal arrangements with other member agencies
- ❏ Coupons
- ❏ Voting privileges
- ❏ Networking opportunities
- ❏ Special volunteer opportunities
- ❏ Consideration for special awards

105 Creative Recognition Idea

Why not integrate monthly (or quarterly) "break bread" dinners into your volunteer recognition efforts? Invite as many as 10 volunteers for an evening of no-pressure shop talk with you, the CEO or key board members. Do it in a social setting (e.g., a local eating establishment) — with no real agenda.

106 Nurture First-time Volunteers

It's smart to publicize the names of first-time volunteers in your newsletter, publicly thanking them for their time and talent. But take it a step further: when that issue is printed, send them an advance copy along with a handwritten note of thanks. The extra personal touch will get their attention.

107 New Benefits Can Lead to Growth

Offering new member benefits sets the stage for fresh growth in an organization.

The La Crosse Community Theatre (LCT) of La Crosse, WI began new patron benefits for its 2006-2007 season. The offerings offset the downside of success, including turning away would-be theatergoers because season ticket holders take up most of the seats.

The organization has been around for 43 years and has consistently had a large, loyal base of season ticket holders and donors. "Approximately 65 to 70 percent of our seating capacity is season ticket holders," says Sandi Ceason Weber, business manager. "Most community theaters can't even dream of that number."

Now LCT is focusing on the future with new staff, including a director of philanthropy. The organization is also looking for a new, larger theater to accommodate more members. It's the perfect time for LCT to start pushing for growth with new member benefits.

New benefits include:

- **Patron Pick:** Give the audience what they want. A survey gives patrons a chance to say what they would like to see on stage. LCT hopes it's an incentive for new people to join as well.

- **Patron Gala:** Show appreciation to patrons with an invitation-only social event. Plans include a recap performance of the past season with drinks and hors d'oeuvres.

- **Bring-a-friend Card:** Reward patrons for their generosity and support. They receive a card allowing them to bring two guests to a performance. "We're confident that many people who are introduced to LCT by friends are going to want to come back again," Ceason Weber says.

Source: Sandi Ceason Weber, Business Manager, La Crosse Community Theatre, La Crosse, WI. Phone (608) 784-9292. E-mail: SCWeber@lacrossecommunitytheatre.org

108 Five Ways to Sustain Memberships

Does it seem like member retention is a recurring battle? Here are five ways to reduce the headache when renewal time approaches:

1. Search your database for members who have yet to renew to find out if any were gift members. Have those members who gave the gift memberships contact the member, either by phone, e-mail or letter, to encourage them to renew.
2. Before sending your first renewal notices, send a letter from the president that recounts successful initiatives from the past year, thanks members for their support of the organization and looks forward to the next year.
3. Include testimonials from members who let their membership lapse, but came back, and how continuing their membership has been of value to them.
4. Offer an incentive (e.g., a dues discount, a logo pen) to members willing to renew with their first renewal notice.
5. Communicate with members regularly, highlighting a new member benefit each time.

109 Member Retention Program a Success

Faced with declining interest in membership among newer resident physicians, the American Academy of Family Physicians (AAFP) of Shawnee Mission, KS began a pilot member retention program called "Experience the AAFP."

The purpose of the program was to get new physician members in their first seven years of residency engaged in AAFP by offering them a sample of CME tools and networking opportunities. They received a $100 discount to the AAFP's annual Scientific Assembly; $100 off a Family Medicine Board Review course or self-study product; $50 off a Family Medicine Board Review Express course; a fellowship at the New Physicians Luncheon at the Scientific Assembly; and several anthologies and CME offerings at a reduced cost or free, says Colleen Lawler, director, AAFP Membership Division.

"The program was very successful," she says. "Those who became engaged — used our services, participated in CME, gave information for their member profile, read our journals — had a higher retention rate and higher satisfaction rate. We were able to increase participation by these members in our annual meeting significantly, and increase their participation in our CME courses and home study program. Retention happens because of member satisfaction with your organization. You have to get them involved before you can get them to stay."

New physicians felt that AAFP recognized what they needed and took the time to provide it, says Lawler: "This program, they said, helped them through what could have been a very challenging part of their career."

Lawler says they got the word out about the program through an extensive communication plan that included the following elements:

- Identifying new physicians
- Communicating with them through a printed piece that explained the program and the new resources
- An e-mail letter signed by an AAFP board of director, who is a new physician
- A monthly newsletter

- A new communication listserv. The new physician board member puts comments up on the listserv about the program.

"In the pilot, we asked new physicians to complete a mini-survey when they requested their free resources," she says. "The survey had a 60 percent response rate."

Source: Colleen Lawler, Director, AAFP Membership Division, American Academy of Family Physicians, Shawnee Mission, KS. Phone (913) 906-6237. E-mail: clawler@aafp.org

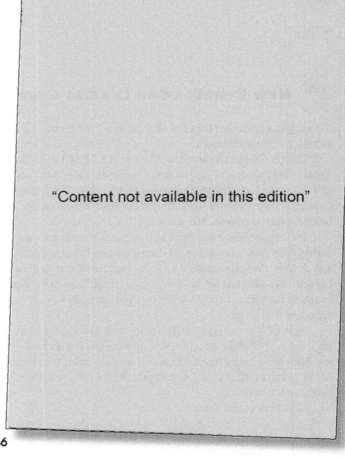
"Content not available in this edition"

Lightning Source UK Ltd.
Milton Keynes UK
UKOW05f1422260516

274943UK00007B/31/P

9 781118 693179